ESSAYS

IN

LITERARY INTERPRETATION

John Keats.

ESSAYS IN LITERARY INTERPRETATION BY HAMILTON WRIGHT MABIE

Library of Congress Cataloging in Publication Data

Mabie, Hamilton Wright, 1846-1916.
Essays in literary interpretation.

(Essay index reprint series)
Reprint of the 1892 ed.
CONTENTS: Some aspects of modern literature.—
Personality in art.—Wordsworth.—The religious theme—
nature in Colridge. [etc.]
1. Literature—Collections. I. Title. II. Series.
PN6014.M25 1972 814′.4′093
72-10734
ISBN 0-8369-6252-4

Essay Index Reprint Series

BOOKS FOR LIBRARIES PRESS
FREEPORT, NEW YORK

First Published 1892
Reprinted 1972

Library of Congress Cataloging in Publication Data

Mabie, Hamilton Wright, 1846-1916.
   Essays in literary interpretation.

   (Essay index reprint series)
   Reprint of the 1892 ed.
   CONTENTS: Some aspects of modern literature.--
Personality in literary work.--The significance of
modern criticism. [etc.]
   1. Literature--Addresses, essays, lectures.
I. Title.
PN511.M15 1972   809   72-293
ISBN 0-8369-2802-4

PRINTED IN THE UNITED STATES OF AMERICA
BY
NEW WORLD BOOK MANUFACTURING CO., INC.
HALLANDALE, FLORIDA 33009

To my Classmates and Friends,

G. STANLEY HALL

AND

FRANCIS LYNDE STETSON.

CONTENTS.

ESSAYS

IN

LITERARY INTERPRETATION.

———◆———

SOME ASPECTS OF MODERN LITERATURE.

MR. ANDREW LANG, in a recent article on the
Greek Anthology, reminds us that in many of these
fragments of a rich and varied literature we come
upon lines full of the modern spirit. The large
objective manner of the earlier poets has given place
to an introspective mood significant of a deepening
self-consciousness, and the remote epic themes have
been succeeded by subjects more intimate and personal. It is true that no period of literature is wholly
destitute of glimpses into familiar life, of disclosures
of personal experience; but when the epic and the
drama are in the ascendant, these are incidental and
subordinate. The great emotions and convictions are
presented in types and symbols; multitudes of persons
are represented by colossal figures, the range and
compass of whose lives create an impression of
universality. The pyramids are race monuments;
they have preserved no record of the individual hard-

I

ship and sacrifice involved in their construction. In like manner the Book of Job, " Prometheus Bound," " Œdipus Tyrannus," and the " Cid " perpetuate ages of personal experience and achievement in commanding types of human nature. The personal element is the very substance of which these typical men and women are formed; but art has discarded that which was individual, in its instinctive search for those qualities which are of universal moment and significance. The personal element enters as substance, but not as form, in the earlier literatures; the individual is of value only as he contributes to those ideal conceptions which live and act in epic remoteness from common life. The mountains are of the same substance as the plain; but on their summits the shepherd's pipe is not heard, nor are the sheep housed there.

We note here one of the most striking differences between the literature of comparatively modern origin and that of earlier periods. The books of this century, contrasted with those of preceding centuries, present a greatly increased complexity of motives, moods, themes, situations. Probably not‧ one phase of experience of any significance has escaped record at the hands of poet, novelist, essayist, or critic. Never before has there been such a universal confession of sins to a confessor devoid of any power of absolution; never before such a complete and outspoken revelation of the things which belong to our most secret lives. The old declaration that there is nothing hidden which shall not be revealed is already fulfilled in our hearing. Those of us who read books must be slow of mind and of heart if we have missed a real and vital knowledge of the age in which, and the men among whom, we live. An impartial spirit of revelation presides over the world of our time and uncovers the unclean and the loathsome as persistently as the pure and the good. The selective principle of the older art has given place to a profound passion for knowledge of life; we are determined to know what is in man at all risks to our tastes and our conventional standards. The process is disagreeable, but the fact is significant; and we shall make a great mistake if in our detestation of the methods of some contemporary writers we refuse to see the meaning of their appearance and activity.

Literature is so closely related to the whole movement of life that every decided tendency which it discloses, every dominant impulse which it reveals, may be studied with the certainty that some fact of human experience, some energy of human purpose and desire, lies behind. The reflection of moving stars and overhanging trees in the depths of still waters is not more perfect than the reproduction of the thoughts and aims and passions of a generation in the books it writes and reads. This conception of the indissoluble union of literature and life is no longer novel and startling to us; but we have so recently come to understand it that we have not yet

fully grasped all there is in it of suggestive and fruitful truth.   Not until we have finally and forever
abandoned the old conception of literature as an art
conformed to certain fixed and final standards shall
we learn the deepest things which books have to
teach us.   So long as we conceive of literature as an
art whose limitations and methods have been established for all time, we shall have small comprehension of modern literature, very imperfect sympathy
with it, and a very inadequate conception of its meaning and its tendency.

Compared with the literature of earlier periods,
modern books, as has been said, show distinctly and
obviously an immensely increased complexity of form
and spirit; the passion for truth and for expression
has become so general and so powerful that it has
burst many ancient channels and made countless new
courses for itself.   Literature to-day tells the whole
truth so far as it knows it; formerly it told only such
truths as were consistent with certain theories of art.
If a modern artist were to paint the parting of Agamemnon and Iphigenia, he would tell the whole story
in the agony of the father's face ; the Greek artist,
on the other hand, veiled the father's anguish in order
that the high tranquillity of art might not be disturbed.
When Agamemnon was murdered, or Œdipus with
his own hand put out his eyes that they might not be
the unwilling witnesses of his doom, the theatre knew
only by report that these events had taken place ;
to-day the whole direful course of the tragedy is

wrought out in full view of the spectators. It may be urged that this removal of the old limits of proper representation in art marks a decadence of the art spirit, a loss of the instinct which set impalpable bounds to the work of the imagination. But it is evident that this expansion of the scope of artistic representation has not been consciously brought about by men who have worked to a common end and bequeathed to their intellectual successors a tradition of iconoclasm. The change has come so slowly and so inevitably that it must be recognized as a universal movement, — the working out of impulses and instincts which are a part of universal human nature, and, therefore, normal and necessary. Great literary movements are never consciously directed; they are always the expression through art of some fresh energy of conviction, some new and large hope and passion of a race or an epoch. The general development of literature is, therefore, in its main directions inevitable and beneficent; if it were not so, progress would be a blunder and life a stagnant pool rather than a running stream.

While there have been periods of decadence, we must assume that the unfolding of the literary power and faculty has been progressive, and has taken place under laws whose operation has been above and beyond human control. Men have spoken through all the forms of art thoughts of whose origin and final outcome they have known as little as one knows of the ports from which and to which

the vessels sail as they come and go against the blue
of the offing. The expansion of the field of literature has not been a matter of choice; it has been
a matter of necessity, and our chief concern is to
accept it as a revelation of the general order under
which we live, and to seek to understand the meaning of it. Students of literature know that when they
come upon a period of large and fruitful activity, they
will find the literary movement contemporaneous
with some widespread and vital movement of thought,
some profound stirring of the depths of popular life.
Without the unusual enrichment of soil, the sudden
and affluent fertility never takes place. If the English people had not been charged with an outpouring
of national spirit strong enough to invigorate English
life from the Strand to the Spanish Main, the great
drama of Shakespeare and his fellow-craftsmen would
not have been written. If literature has been vastly
extended, it has been because the literary impulse
has made itself more generally felt. Formerly a few
men and women wrote the books of the world. They
were the voices of a silent world; as we listen, we
seem at first to hear no other words but theirs. We
might hastily conclude that there were no thoughts in
those old times but those that come to us from a few
lips, musical with an eloquence which charms time
itself into silence and memory. These great souls
must surely have been of other substance than the
countless multitudes who died and gave no sound;
remote from the lost and forgotten civilizations which

surrounded them, they breathed a larger air and moved with the gods. But as we listen more intently and patiently, these puissant tones seem to issue from a world-wide inarticulate murmur; they are no longer solitary; they interpret that which lies unspoken in countless hearts. How solitary Job sits among his griefs as we look back upon him! All the races who dwelt about him have vanished; the world of activity and thought in which he lived has perished utterly; but there stands the immortal singer with that marvellous song, — "sublime sorrow, sublime reconciliation; oldest choral melody as of the heart of mankind; so soft and great; as the summer midnight, as the world with its seas and stars." But this sublime argument, which moves on with such a sweep of wing, is not the thought of Job alone; it is the groping, doubting aspiration of the East finding voice and measure for itself; it is the movement of the mind of a people through its long search for truth; it is the spiritual history of a race. The lonely thinker, under those clear Eastern skies, made himself the interpreter of the world which he alone has survived. Back of the great poem there is an unwritten history greater and more pathetic than the poem itself, could we but uncover it.

Great books are born not in the intellect, but in experience, — in the contact of mind and heart with the great and terrible facts of life; the great conceptions of literature originate not in the individual mind, but in the soil of common human hopes, loves, fears,

aspirations, sufferings.   Shakespeare did not invent
Hamlet; he found him in human histories already
acted out to the tragic end.   Goethe did not create
Faust; he summoned him out of the dim mediæval
world, brought him face to face with the crucial experiences of life, and so fashioned a character and
a career which have become typical.   "It takes a
great deal of life," said Alfred de Musset, "to make
a little art."   The more deeply we study great books
the more clear it becomes that literature is not primarily an art born of skill and training, but the expression of man's growth into comprehension of his
own life and of the sublime order of which he is part.
Life itself is the final fact for which all men of genuine gift and insight are searching; and the great books
are either representations or interpretations of this
all-embracing fact.   There are wide differences of
original endowment, of temperament, of training, of
environment.   There are broad contrasts of spirit,
method, treatment; but a common impulse underlies
all great works of literary genius.   When Byron, with
a few daring strokes, draws the portrait of Manfred,
when Wordsworth meditates among the Cumberland
Hills, each in his way draws near to life, — the one
to picture and the other to interpret it.   No rapt and
lonely vision lifts them to heights inaccessible to
common thought and need; their gift of insight,
while it separates them from their fellows as individuals, unites them the more closely with humanity.
For the essential greatness of men of genius does not

lie in their separation from their fellows, nor in any moods which are peculiarly their own, but in that inexplicable union of heart and mind which makes them sharers of the private life of the world, discerners of that which is hidden in individual experience, interpreters of men to themselves and to each other.

The great mass of men arrive late at complete self-consciousness, at a full knowledge of themselves. The earlier generations attained this self-knowledge for the most part very imperfectly; it was the possession of a few, and these elect souls spoke for the uncounted hosts of their silent contemporaries. When any considerable number of individuals of the same race secured this complete possession of themselves, there was a wide and adequate expression of life as they saw it. By virtue of natural aptitude, of exceptional opportunity for knowing what is in life, and of a training of a very high and complete kind, the Greeks attained a degree of self-knowledge which was far in advance of the attainment of most of the Oriental races. This mastery of life and its arts was disclosed chiefly in one city, and within a single century that city enriched literature for all time by a series of masterpieces. If there had been elsewhere the same degree of self-knowledge, there would have been a corresponding impulse toward expression. But except among the Hebrews, there was not; for the most part the races in the East contemporaneous with the Greeks did not attain anything more than a very inadequate conception of themselves and their relation to the world.   Among the Hindoos there was, it is true, a very considerable and a very noble literary development; but this movement for expression was partial and inadequate because the knowledge that inspired it was partial and inadequate.   The Hindoos entangled God in the shining meshes of his own creation; they never clearly separated him in thought from Nature, and they never perfectly realized their own individuality.   The great Western races, on the other hand, were so absorbed in the vast activities of growth and empire that they had small inclination to study themselves; the Romans conquered the world, but when it lay within their grasp, they did not know what to do with it, so inadequate was their knowledge of themselves and of the real nature of their possessions.   The literature of such a people will rarely reveal any original impulse or force; it will not even express the consciousness of power, which is more clearly realized than anything else by such a people; it will be an imitative art, whose chief attraction will lie in the natural or acquired skill of individuals, and whose chief use will be to register great deeds, not to express and illustrate great souls and a great common life.   The Northern races, whose various stages of growth were to be recorded in noble literary forms, were still in the period of childhood, and knew neither their own strength nor the weakness of the older civilization which surrounded them.

During periods of imperfect self-knowledge there

will be necessarily fewer thoughts, convictions, or emotions to inspire expression ; and these will be clearly felt and adequately uttered by a few persons. The simplicity of life in such periods makes a very massive and noble art possible ; such an art as the Greeks created as a revelation of their own nature and an expression of their thought about themselves and the world. The limitations of such an art give it definiteness, clearness of outline, large repose and harmony. And these limitations are not imposed as a matter of artifice; they are in large measure unconscious, and they are, therefore, inevitable. To impose the standards and boundaries of the art of such a period upon the art of later and immensely expanded periods would be as irrational as to impose on the America of to-day the methods of the America of the colonial period.

As self-knowledge becomes the possession of a larger number of persons, becomes general rather than individual, the faculty of expression is correspondingly developed until the gift and office of the fortunate few become almost public functions. Apollo's lyre still yields its supreme melodies to the greatest souls only, but a host have learned to set their thought to its lighter strains. Now, it is precisely this general development of self-knowledge which characterizes our modern life and reveals itself in our varied and immensely diversified literature. Humanity has come to a large measure of maturity. It has had a long history, which has been the record of its efforts to know

its own nature and to master the field and the imple-
ments of its activity.   It has made countless experi-
ments, and has learned quite as much from its failures
as from its successes.   It has laboriously traversed
the island in space where its fortunes are cast ; it has
listened intently, generation after generation, for some
message from beyond the seas which encompass it.
It has made every kind of venture to enlarge its capital of pleasure, and it has hazarded all its gains for
some nobler fortune of which it has dreamed.   It has
opened its arms to receive the joys of life, and missing
them, has patiently clasped a crucifix.   It has drank
every cup of experience ; won all victories and suffered all defeats ; tested all creeds and acted all philosophies ; illustrated all baseness and risen to the
heights of all nobleness.   In short, humanity has lived,
— not in a few persons, a few periods, a few activities,
but in countless persons, through long centuries, and
under all conditions.   Surely some larger and more
comprehensive idea of life lies in the mind of the
modern world than ever defined itself to the men of
the earlier times.   Society has still much to learn ;
but men have now lived long enough to have attained
a fairly complete self-knowledge.   They have by no
means fully developed themselves, but they know
what is in them.   Humanity has come to maturity,
and to the self-consciousness which is the power of
maturity.

With this self-consciousness there has come a corresponding power of expression ; the two are as in-

separable as the genius of the composer and the music through which it reveals itself, as the impulse of the sculptor and the carven stone in which it stands expressed. Thought and expression are parts of one complete act. As conceptions of life multiply and widen, language is unconsciously expanded and enriched to receive and convey them ; as experience deepens, speech matches it with profounder and subtiler phrase. With the power to communicate that which is essentially novel comes also the impulse. Expression is the habit and the law of civilized life. There is within us an instinctive recognition of the universal quality of thought and experience ; we feel that neither can be in any sense our private possession. They belong to the world, and even when we endeavour to keep them to ourselves they seem to elude and escape us. No sooner does one utter a thought that was new to him than a hundred other men claim a common ownership with him. It was, as we say, in the air, and he had unconsciously appropriated that which was public property. There is a large and noble consistency behind our fragmentary thinking which makes us aware of some great order of things with which we are unconsciously working. Our lesser thought is always seen in the end to be part of a larger thought. The investigator, working along one line of scientific research, finds his latest discovery of that which seemed the special law of his department matched by the discovery of the same law operating in an entirely different field. Men of large

vision know that the same general tendencies are discoverable at almost any given time in science, art,
philosophy, literature, and theology.   The significance
of these common tendencies is deepened by the fact
that for the most part the individual workers in the
different fields are unconscious of them.   They are all
unwitting witnesses to a higher and more comprehensive truth than that which each is bent upon demon-
strating.   There is, in other words, a continuous
revelation of ultimate things through the totality of
human activity and experience ; and this revelation,
which is co-extensive with universal life, presses upon
men for expression.   Whether they will or not, it
must utter itself; behind all life it sets its mighty impulse, and nothing can resist it.   With the immense
expansion of modern life it was inevitable that there
should be an immense expansion of literature ; that
new literary forms like the novel should be developed ;
that facts hitherto suppressed or unobserved should
be brought to light ; and that phases and aspects of
experience hitherto unrecorded should suddenly en-
shrine themselves in art.

The broadening of the literary impulse, the impulse
of expression, has materially changed the prevailing
character of literature and indefinitely multiplied its
forms.   Instead of commanding types, massive because isolated, there has succeeded a vast variety of
more specialized types, in which the great truths of
experience, instead of being generalized into a few
personalities, are dispersed through many.   Literature

no longer reveals only the summits of thought and action ; it displays the whole landscape of life,— continent and sea, barren wilderness and blossoming field, lonely valley and shining peak. Personality is no longer sublimated in order to present its universal elements ; it is depicted in its most familiar and intimate forms. In art Raphael's Madonnas and Michael Angelo's colossal figures have been succeeded by Bastien-Lepage's Jean d'Arc and Millet's Angelus, — not because the religious feeling is less penetrating and profound, but because it recognizes in nearer and more familiar forms the sanctity and dignity it once saw only in things most beautiful and august. Under the same impulse the literary instinct seeks to discover what is significant in the life that is nearest, convinced that all life is a revelation, and that to the artist beauty is universally diffused through all created things. As the wayside flower, once neglected, discloses a loveliness all its own, so does the human thought, emotion, experience, once passed by in the pursuit of some remoter theme. Literature, which holds so vital a relation to the inner life of men, shows in this more catholic and sympathetic selection of characters and scenes the new and deeper conception of human relationship which is now the most potent factor in the social life of the world.

One looks in vain through the earlier literatures for such frank disclosures of personal feeling and habit, such unveiling of self, as are found in Montaigne, Cellini, Rousseau, and Amiel. But these direct and explicit confessions are hardly more personal and individual than the great mass of modern literature. We know the secret thoughts, the hidden processes of character, in Tito and Anna Karénina, even more completely than if these creations, become actual flesh and blood, had attempted to give us their confidence. The great writers who have drawn these masterly portraits have comprehended the significance of the almost imperceptible stages by which motives and impulses are moved forward to their ultimate issue in action, by which character is advanced from its plastic to its final and permanent form. They have seen that dramatic interest does not attach exclusively to those well-defined climaxes of experience which we call crises, but invests and gives artistic value to the whole movement of life ; that no acts which have moral or intellectual quality are unimportant. The peasant is quite as interesting a figure to the literary artist as the king ; has become, in fact, far more attractive and suggestive, since nothing intervenes between him and human nature in its purest form. Interest in the great fact of life has become so intense that we are impatient of all the conventions and traditions that conceal it from us. The novels to-day are full of studies of men and women in the most primitive conditions and relations, and he must command the very highest resources of his art who would interest us in a character swathed in the trappings of royalty. These things seem tawdry and unreal to a generation that has caught a glimpse of the awful meaning of life as it works out its purpose in every individual soul. If Shakespeare were living to-day, his Lear might not be an uncrowned king, but the kinsman of that lonely, massive peasant-figure whose essential and tragic dignity Tourguenieff has made so impressive in "The Lear of the Steppes." Genius is the highest form of sympathy; and in modern literature this quality has made it the interpreter of the complete experience of humanity. It has been irresistibly °drawn to that which is lowly and obscure because it has discerned in these untrodden paths a beauty and a meaning essentially new to men; it has become conscious of the pathetic contrast between souls encompassed with limitations and the eternal elements of which they are compounded.

They must be blind indeed who fail to discover in this attitude of literature toward men and women as individuals a change of thought as vital as any that ever has taken place in history. The commonest life is touched and irradiated by this spirit of insight, and in the lowliest as in the most impressive person and fact, an inexhaustible significance is discovered. Literature has come close to life not only in its great historic manifestations, but in its most familiar and homely aspects, and it lends itself with impartial sympathy to the portrayal and interpretation of both. The phrase whose novel appeal to a common humanity once brought out the applause of the Roman theatre is to-day written as a supreme law across all our arts. Nothing that is human is insignificant or without

2

interest for us. Our common search is not for theories of life, — they are all being cast aside because
they are all inadequate, — but for the facts of life.
There is coming at last the dawn of a great and
worthy thought of this life of ours, and the universe in
which it is set; and as this thought clears itself from
imperfect knowledge and from ancient ignorance, a
new reverence for the humblest human soul is born
within us. The expansion of man's conception of
the universe from the time of Ptolemy to that of
Tyndall has not been greater than the expansion of
the conception of the meaning of life from the thought
of the first or the thirteenth century to that of the
nineteenth century. One result of this vaster conception of life is the recognition of its supremacy over
the arts. They were once ends in themselves; they
are now means of expression. They were once supreme and final achievements; they are now records
and registers of that which is greater than they.

Art is the necessary and universal quality of literature; it is the presence or absence of this quality
which elects some books for long life and others for
the life of a day. It is the impalpable and subtile
touch of art which confers on a book, a picture, or a
statue that longevity which we rashly call immortality.
But as books accumulate, and as the years multiply
into centuries and the centuries lengthen into epochs,
we become conscious of the impotence of art itself
to elude the action of that change from a lower to
a higher form which we call death. There are no

finalities of expression ; life has always a new word to
utter, a new form to fashion. The greatest cannot
hope to measure the complete span of a single age,
much less the span of all history. We shall not think
less of our arts, but we are coming to have a new
thought about them. The men who create them are
greater than they ; humanity is greater than the sum
of all its achievements and expressions. Art must
come closer to us, must be more reverent and humble,
must be our servant and not master. Literature is
already full of the signs of this change. It has suffered no real loss in the evolution through which it
has passed from a few simple and impressive forms
to an expression at once more flexible and of vastly
increased volume. If the great chords that once
vibrated to an infrequent hand are now less distinct
and commanding, it is because the lyre yields its
full harmony to the passionate touch of life.

PERSONALITY IN LITERARY WORK.

DR. JOHNSON is probably the best English illustration of a writer whose personality was so inadequately expressed in his work that what he was is likely to obliterate what he did. The man was hearty, simple, often offensively, always unaffectedly, forceful and downright; his work, on the other hand, while sound and wholesome, is formal, academic, elaborate, and at times highly artificial. No man spoke with more resolute Saxon bluntness than the author of those solemn and imposing essays in the "Rambler," of whom Goldsmith said that if he wrote of little fishes they would all speak like great whales. That his pen was not wholly devoid of the vigour which his speech uniformly had, is evident to every one who reads his letters; but as a rule this rugged strength is diffused and lost in a succession of well-wrought phrases rather than concentrated on the sharp edge of concise and telling sentences. It is certainly no lack of personality which one feels in reading Johnson; the Doctor is never far off in those infrequent moments when one takes up "Rasselas" or the "Rambler;" but it is the wigged and powdered professional man of letters in the wigged and powdered eighteenth century, not the big-brained, big-hearted, irascible, pathetic, and unaffectedly human hero of Boswell's immortal biography. In the whole company of English writers from Chaucer to Carlyle there is no more sharply defined and vigorous personality; none more pronounced, more clearly shown, more easily understood. Evidently the failure of Johnson's work to impress us adequately is in no sense due to lack of individuality behind it; the fact that we are transferring our interest more and more from the work to the man shows clearly enough that the man possessed qualities which his work fails to convey. Johnson's defect as a writer lay in his inability to make his voice distinct; it does not ring clear in perfectly natural tones. When he talked, his words were charged with the electric current of his tremendous personality; when he wrote, the circuit was broken; at some point the current escaped into the air, and the reader never receives any emotion or impulse approaching a shock in intensity. It is probable that the only saving quality in Johnson's work is due to the fact that it helps us to understand him. In most cases we remember the man because of the work he did; in Johnson's case we shall remember the work because of the man who did it.

Shakespeare, on the other hand, furnishes the best English illustration of a writer whose personality is completely expressed in his work. The work we know by heart; of the man we know almost nothing in the sense that we know Dr. Johnson. So slight and fragmentary is our knowledge of the outward facts of Shakespeare's life that this noblest of modern minds has furnished the material for the most fantastic exercise of arbitrary inference known in the history of literature. If Shakespeare had had his Boswell, we might have possessed an authoritative history of " Hamlet " and the " Tempest," — something which would have given us the order and sequence of these marvellous plays. They are creations, however, not pieces of mechanism ; and nothing deeper could be told about them than they reveal themselves. About every great work of art there is something mysterious and inexplicable ; and he who can explain it least is he by whose hand it was done. Shakespeare's spiritual autobiography lies clearly written in his work, although the aspect under which his contemporaries knew him is barely hinted at there. Shakespeare's Boswell would have been intensely interesting ; we could well have spared libraries of commentaries if his single volume could have taken their place ; but he could have rendered no such service to his master or to us as Johnson's Boswell performed. Johnson spoke from the surface of his nature when he set hand to paper, and the gleanings of Boswell were more than the harvester gathered ; Shakespeare spoke from the depths of his nature and in all the tones which impart expression to uttered speech, and a Boswell would have found little unsaid that was needed to the complete expression of his spiritual nature. It would have given us deep satisfaction to have known something of his smile, his carriage, his manner of speech and bearing among his fellows; but we know from his own report his thought of human life, encircled by mysteries, swayed by the winds of passion, calmed by the weight of its own destiny; and the essential thing to be known about any man is his thought about these matters.

These two writers will serve to illustrate a principle which becomes clearer the more thoroughly and widely we apply it to all works which belong distinctively to literature : the principle that a man's work approaches the very highest standard in the degree in which it expresses his personality, — personality in the large sense which includes temperament, quality of imagination, artistic sense, point of view, education, and faculty of expression. The word is often used to express what is obvious and idiosyncratic in a man's nature or history; and literary work is sometimes said to be full of personality when it is stamped with this kind of individual quality. The idea of personality implied in this criticism is not false, but it is inadequate; and it becomes misleading when it is applied as a test. "The Sorrows of Werther," "Obermann," and Rousseau's "Confessions" are charged with an intensity of mood or emotion which conveys a vivid impression of personality; but the real Goethe is to be sought elsewhere than in the "Sorrows of Werther," — the rounded and full personality of the man is not only concealed, but misrepresented, by the momentary passion which burned itself out in that work of his youth. These intense expressions of critical moments in a man's growth, these cries out of the heart of a passing anguish, are indeed charged with personality, but with a personality limited in time and experience; they are not the complete and harmonious expression of the whole man. If we seek this, we shall find it not in these passionate outcries, but in the clear, strong, harmonic tones that convey the full significance of deep, rich, masterful life and thought. The personality of Byron, of Leopardi, of De Musset, is so obvious, so interesting, so pungent, that their work and the work of men of their class seem like the truest and deepest expression of the man behind it; its intensity makes the calmness and range of the greatest writers seem entirely impersonal. When, however, we study these larger and more varied creations, we find ourselves in the presence of men whose restraint and repose are significant not of repression, but of free, complete, and beautiful self-expression. It is in Sophocles, in Shakespeare, in Molière, in Goethe, that we find the ripest and most powerful personalities, — personalities that have not rested in simple transcriptions of the feeling of the moment, but have made their own experiences illustrative of universal law, and in the untroubled surface of their calm, deep natures have·reflected the whole moving image of things. "Manfred," "The Robbers," and "Queen Mab" are not defective in disclosure of personality; but in all works of their kind the personality is either limited in time or in expe-

rience ; it is a personality narrow in itself or imperfectly expressed. If a man is to make the most of
his materials, he must have that mastery of them
which permits him to transpose and combine them at
will; which makes them pliant and flexible in his
hand. This apt and varied skill eludes those who,
by the limitation of their own natures or the violence
of their emotions, are driven rather than inspired by
the critical moment and experience. The artist is
most inspired when his hand is freest and surest, because intensity and agitation of emotion have passed
on into depth and clearness of vision.

Personality in the larger sense is to be found not
in what is strongly individualistic in temper and
expression, but in what is distinctive and characteristic
in a man's view of life and art, — in his structural
force and genius; in the quality and direction of his
insight ; in the adequacy and inevitableness of his
expression. At the very bottom of a man's work lies
his thought of life, — his idea of the materials which
are at hand and of the use he can make of them ;
and this thought contains the very essence of that
which makes the man different from all other men
who have been or shall be. For this thought
embodies everything that is peculiar and distinctive
to him. The thought of a mature man about life and
art is the adjustment of the man's self to the world
which he finds about him ; when he has reached a
conception of the significance of life and the uses of
art, he has determined that which is most fundamental

for himself and most deeply and permanently definitive of his character and genius. The conception may be primarily moral, philosophic, artistic; it may involve clear insight into the lines of right, of thought, or of beauty along which the universe is built; whatever it is, it determines the genius of the man and sets him apart to express once and forever a thought which is essentially his own. Centuries have passed since the first great dramatic poems were written; and yet neither Job nor Æschylus, neither Shakespeare nor Molière, has been repeated. Every dramatist of the first order has had a fundamental thought about life which, expressed in his own way, has been in some essential things different from the thought of all his fellows; and that thought has contained the very essence of his personality. The great writers speak not from report, but from personal knowledge. They differ from the lesser writers not only in quality of workmanship, but still more in the fact that they are witnesses of the truth which they express. They have seen and felt; therefore they speak. And that which thus sees and feels and knows is the man's whole nature, not observation only, nor thought only, nor feeling only. All the faculties, the aptitudes, the sensibilities, the experiences which make us what we are, are involved in this process. So that which lies deepest in a man, his thought of the movement of things in which he finds himself, expresses completely and most profoundly his personality.

There are some elements in this personality which we can distinguish and trace. There are racial marks on the mind and temperament of every man; there are evident impressions of the time in which he lives, with all its subtile and interwoven influences; but however keenly we distinguish these secondary qualities, and however acutely we analyze them, we never uncover the secret of personality. That is a thing which is primary, and cannot be resolved into its elements, — a thing which is vital and cannot be comprehended. We learn more and more of the vital processes, but we never overtake life itself; we get nearer and nearer to the secret of genius, but we never lay our hand on it. There is something in us that cometh not by observation and that escapes our scrutiny; and this sacred and inaccessible thing, which the most searching science is powerless to wrest from a man, is what he gives us in a great piece of art. Every great piece of art expresses a great thought, and in that thought is summed up the totality of a man's nature and life.

This thought, as has been said, is not primarily the result of a conscious process of thinking. It comes to a man he knows not how; in swift flashes of intelligence, in the sudden illumination of experience, in the long silence of brooding, under the pressure of tremendous experiences. It is distilled into a man's soul by the alchemy of living, — that mysterious process by which, through thought, emotion, and action, we attain both knowledge and character.

The frankest autobiographies always leave unsaid the thing we care most to know; they give us hints, side-lights, pregnant suggestions, but they always leave a residuum of mystery. No man was ever yet perfectly explained to his fellows; and no man ever will be. We shall know some men far more thoroughly than we know others, but we shall never know any man completely. Nor will any man ever attain complete self-knowledge, — that kind of knowledge which will disclose all the sources of his power, trace back every rivulet of influence to its ancestral spring, uncover all the depths not only of personal but of inherited experience, make clear what he receives from his own time, and mark that which is distinctively his own; that residuum which neither time, race, nor circumstances account for. In every soul, as in every life, there is something solitary and incommunicable, — a holy of holies upon which the veil is never lifted. It is written that no man can see God and live; and there is something divine in us upon which we are not suffered to look. It is this mysterious and essential personality, modified in expression by the temporary elements of place and age, but fundamentally apart from and independent of them, which inspires and gives form to every great work of art; so that there is in every masterpiece something inexplicable, — something which cannot be referred to anything anterior; something, in a word, which we call creative because we cannot account for it in any other way. An imitative work discloses its parentage :

a creative work stands apart and remains mute when we question its ancestry. It is surrounded by the same mystery which enfolds every birth, which attaches to everything that is born, not made.

The work is mysterious even to its creator. "The soul," says Calvert, "while laying the foundations of greatness, keeps its own counsel; and what it has been doing and preparing is only revealed by the completed work." It is a very suggestive fact that Goethe could never explain many things in "Faust." They were there, and that was about the substance of his knowledge of them. Few literary works have been so long in hand, have been so often taken up and laid aside, have received such constant and long-continued revision. Of the outward history of few poems do we know so much; and yet there was much in it which Goethe confessed himself unable to account for. The origin of the work itself was as mysterious to him as to every one else. It is easy enough to indicate the sources of the legend and of many of the incidents woven into it; but what affinity lodged this seed in the soil of his nature, what were the stages by which it sank deep into his soul and became so thoroughly part of himself that it came forth from his brain not only re-fashioned, amplified, harmonized with itself in artistic consistency, but pervaded by a soul which made it significant of profound and universal truth? "I can truly say of my production," said Goethe, referring to his drama of "Tasso," "it is bone of my bone and flesh of my flesh. . . . They come and ask what idea I meant to embody in my 'Faust,' as if I knew myself and could inform them." For more than sixty years the drama was on his mind ; and yet he tells us that the whole poem rose before him at once when it first touched his imagination. He often spoke of the progress of the work ; there are, indeed, few works of art concerning the shaping and evolution of which we possess such full and trustworthy information ; and yet of the first contract between the idea and his own soul, all he can tell us is that it was suddenly and completely disclosed to his imagination. His inability to explain it was not due to lack of an underlying motive or to vagueness and obscurity of idea, but to the fact that he did not consciously originate it ; it came to him, and he gave it form. The story of Goethe's masterpiece is the story of every masterpiece ; there are interesting facts in every such story, but the essential fact, the fact that would have explained the work, is always missing ; no man can furnish it, because no man's knowledge has ever compassed it. Every such work is the expression of a man's personality ; and personality is a primary and unresolvable force in the world.

Through the alembic of personality pass all the ideas which appear in art ; detached from a personality, an idea may appear as science or philosophy, but it never can appear as art. It is this truth which Mr. James hints at when he says that art is mainly a point of view ; it is that and as much more as one brings to the point of view. Whipple had the same truth in mind when he said that " the measure of a man's individuality is his creative power ; and all that Shakespeare created he individually included." In order to show Romeo the prey of a consuming passion, Shakespeare must have felt the possible heat of a kindred flame ; in order to portray Hamlet bending beneath the awful mystery of life and thought, Shakespeare must have felt the danger of a similar loss of adjustment between meditation and action ; in order to picture Antony casting a world away, he must have known the power of such a spell as that woven on the banks of the Nile. These experiences may not have been actual in the life of the dramatist, but they must all have been possible. They form the universal element in which he works, and they are transformed into art by passing through an artist's personality. No two men ever saw the same rainbow, because no two men ever looked at a rainbow from the same point of view ; life was never the same to any two human hearts, and, in the nature of things, never can be. Æschylus will discern in it a vastness and mystery which will escape the beautiful but distinctively Greek mind of Sophocles ; Marlowe will find in it a violence and excess which will fall below the luminous horizon of Shakespeare's mind ; Corneille will discover in it a rigid and stately order, which in the vital and mobile mind of Molière will give place to a more real and vivid perception of individual characteristics.

The rank of a writer rests in the last analysis on the distinctness and individuality of his thought and of the form which it takes ; and the fuller and more complete the personality of the man, the more powerful and varied will be the work of his hand. A limited experience and restricted insight, like Grey's, mean a work which, despite its supreme quality, is seen to lie within narrow confines ; a rich experience, a broad insight, a limitless intellectual sympathy, like Browning's, necessarily imply a vast range of expression, a creation adequate in scope and variety to the force of the creative impulse. If this power of seeing, this swift capacity of entering into all life, reaches its highest development, we have a Dante compassing a whole epoch of history with his thought, or a Shakespeare speaking out of the heart of entire humanity. They have seen ; they know ; therefore they speak.

There is no such thing as a universal literature in the sense which involves complete escape from all the water-marks of place and time. An expression of thought thus detached would be without structural order and harmony, without colour, atmosphere, style ; would cease to be literature, and become philosophy. The star does not lose the majesty of its movement or the splendour of its aspect because, if we observe it at all, we must observe it from some infinitesimally small point of earth. No man can study or interpret life save from the point of view where he finds himself ; and the range and beauty of vision which he discerns depend upon the clearness and range of his sight. In the deepest sense there are no abstract truths, no worlds swinging in invisible space; that only exists for us at any given time which in some way reaches and touches us, in some way penetrates and affects us. No truth gets into human keeping by any other path than the individual soul, nor into human speech by any other medium than the individual mind. The universal element in literature lies not in its detachment from personality, in its separation from the peculiarities of age, place, and person, but in the completeness and power with which it expresses these things, — for all things partake of the universal, and we have only to pierce the special and particular deep enough, and we shall find it. It is the function of literature to portray and interpret those things which all men understand because they are shared by all men; but both in portrayal and interpretation it is the presence of the art quality which makes the work literature; and this quality is always imparted by personality. Detach the truth embodied in " Hamlet " from the dramatic form in which it is cast, and there remains a series of aphorisms or comments upon character and life; the truth thus expressed is not less true because it has changed its form, but it has ceased to be literature.

Every work of art has an interior order or architecture which in any analysis is hardly less important or significant than the leading conception or idea which it conveys. As a matter of fact, it is impossible to separate the two; in any true work of art they are so perfectly fused and blended that they are no longer separable. When we have detached the thought of " Pippa Passes " or " In Memoriam " from its organic sequence in the poem, we have destroyed the poem. The division is impossible, because it does not exist in the work; and yet, as a matter of convenience and in aid of clearness of thought, arbitrary and artificial distinctions may be used to advantage. The structural quality of a work is something much more essential than the outward form which determines the department of literature to which it belongs. The form is part of it, but part only. The structural quality of the " Divine Comedy " is the very substance of the poem; it is that which gives it its unique place and value. Dante had a clear, profound, and spiritual conception of the soul of man in the vast experience of life. If he had been a philosopher only or distinctively, he would have written a system of theology; but he was a poet of supreme insight and force. He did not meditate upon abstractions; he saw the soul of man in all the manifold stages of its experience; it was not the thought which he pursued, it was the soul with which he walked in all the length of its awful journeying. He did not philosophize about punishment; he breathed the very air and was blown upon by the very flames of hell. He did not theorize about purification; he heard the groans and felt the hot and bitter tears of purgatory. He did not dream about the rewards of righteousness and the blessedness of the good; he heard the in-

effable strains, and covered his face in the glory of
Paradise. The great conception was not first a
system of thought and then a sublime dramatic creation; long purposed, sternly executed, it was never
other than a complete and consuming vision of humanity under the conditions of eternity,— when penalty
does not follow, but is part of sin; when result does
not pursue but accompanies act; when reward and
retribution are realized at the same instant within and
without the soul. That which Dante saw was concrete and indivisible ; it did not come to him in parts,
although it grew into proportion and harmony in his
mind ; he did not put it together as a piece of mechanism, fitting thought to expression and matching
the great inspiring idea with a majestic epic form.
In such a work of art there is no separation of soul
and body; a thing of immortality has no perishable
part. It comes, an indivisible, indestructible creation,
from the soul of the artist ; no sound of hammer was
heard in the making of it, — for, like all great products
of the imagination, it was a creation and a growth, not
a mechanism and a manufacture. Another poet of
Dante's genius, dealing with the same theme, would
have given us a different poem, because he would have
conceived of it in a different way ; and a difference
of construction would have involved a difference of
idea. If one may venture upon philosophic terms,
the moment the idea shapes itself, harmonizes itself,
becomes organic and concrete instead of abstract,
the structural element enters into the process. The

work passes through the pre-natal stages before it is
born in the artist's mind; it is fashioned in that sublime mystery which lies behind all birth. Shall it be
epic, lyric, or drama? is a question which the poet is
never asked. It is already one or the other of these
before it is disclosed to him. By the structure of a
great literary work is meant, therefore, something very
different from its mere form, — something which is of
the very heart and soul of the work; that which brings
it out of the region of abstraction into the world of
human perception and thought; that by which the
ideal enters into and becomes a part of the real.

This structural element is discovered, appropriated,
or furnished by the imagination, — the one creative
faculty we possess, and the "master light of all our
seeing." The more closely we study human knowledge and thought, the more clearly do we perceive
that this word "imagination" has more compass and
depth of meaning than any other word which we
apply to our faculties. It includes all that we possess of constructive power, — the power of holding
masses of facts so firmly and continuously in the
field of vision as to enable us to discover their unity
and the laws which govern them; in other words,
science, — the power of seeing the permanent in the
transitory, the universal in the particular; in other
words, philosophy, — the power of perceiving and realizing the soul of things visible, and out of the real
constructing the ideal; in other words, art, — the
power of discerning the spiritual behind the material,

the creator behind the creation; in other words, religion. Wherever and whenever life becomes great and the world real to us, the imagination holds aloft its quenchless torch. In every hour when a new truth moves back a little the horizon of thought, or a new birth of beauty expands a little the world of art, the imagination is present. " I assert for myself," said William Blake, " that I do not behold the outward creation, and that to me it would be a hindrance and not action. I question not my corporeal eye any more than I would question a window concerning a sight. I look through it, and not with it." It is to the imagination alone that second sight belongs, — that sight which does not rest in obvious and material things, but through them, as through an open window, perceives another and diviner order of creation. Thus the imagination fulfils for the soul the double function of seeing and interpreting, of discovering and possessing.

But the imagination is not simply or mainly an organ of vision ; it is a hand even more than an eye, and a hand which moves to the impulse of inspiration. It was the imagination which discovered the beauty of the world to the earliest men, and it was the imagination which peopled it with the antique gods ; in the history of art seeing and creating have never been dissevered. It is by the activity of the imagination that we possess those masterpieces which, if they fail to convey all that the ideal contains, define for us the laws of beauty and fix the standards of supreme excellence.   If they cannot bring perfection within the range of our senses, they fail not to bring it within the reach of our souls.   Now, the imagination which perceives the idea under some inevitable structural form is not less distinctive and individual than is that mysterious personality which makes a man what he is, as different from all other men. This personality determines the idea that becomes the germ of a great creative work; determines that the story of Prometheus shall belong to Æschylus, and the story of Faust to Goethe, and the conception of Tartuffe to Molière; but it is the imagination which opens the personality to the idea, and by placing it in relation with the visible and actual, brings the material within reach of the shaping hand.   What interior structure the idea shall have, how it shall be shaped, where unite with and where depart from that which art has already achieved, depends on the individual imagination.   Faust will be one thing to Marlowe and an entirely different thing to Goethe, the dominant idea remaining the same; and when we study the differences of structure and treatment between the two dramas, we perceive that we are studying the differences between the two poets.   Between Voltaire's thought of Jean d'Arc in " La Pucelle " and the vision on the canvas of Bastien-Lepage, what an almost measureless divergence of personality is expressed!   If the masters of creative literature are studied by the comparative method, nothing is more striking than the differences which exist between them in quality and force of imagination; and it is such study which enables us to understand that the imagination is the creative faculty.

It is only the most superficial thinking which fails to perceive that style is no less integral, essential, and inevitable than inspiring idea, structural form, or force and quality of imagination. It is obvious that the style of a writer is not uninfluenced by his age: compare the prose of Sir Thomas Malory with that of Milton, that of Fuller with that of Addison, that of Johnson with that of Ruskin or Newman, and the presence of a process of development is unmistakable. It is obvious also that a writer, by that rigid discipline which is the condition of all artistic excellence, may expand and even radically change his style. · Nevertheless, it remains true that the style of a genuine writer is in the deepest sense inevitable, and that all his conscious effort has not fashioned, but found it. It was already existent, to borrow the idea of one of the masters of style, Flaubert; and the whole education of the man in the secrets of his art has been an endeavour to bring together two things which are parts of one whole. "Possessed," says a critic of the author of "Madame Bovary," "of an absolute belief that there exists but one way of expressing one thing, one word to call it by, one adjective to qualify, one verb to animate it, he gave himself to superhuman labour for the discovery, in every phrase, of that word, that verb, that epithet. In this way he believed in some mysterious harmony of expression, and when a true word seemed to him to lack euphony, still went on seeking another with invincible patience, certain that he had not yet got hold of the unique word. . . . A thousand preoccupations would beset him at the same moment, always with this desperate certitude fixed in his spirit, — among all the expressions in the world, all forms and terms of expression, there is but *one* — one form, one mode — to express what I want to say." There is no paradox in all this; for while style is an end which may be consciously worked for, it is also and always, whenever it reaches the highest level of art, a full, free, and powerful expression of personality, and as such it was determined for the man in the hour in which his personality was compounded. The search for style is therefore never a search for something artificial, something so distinct from the searcher that he may choose among several, rejecting one and accepting another; it is always the effort to attain complete self-expression. Some writers never find their true style, and failing of genuine self-expression, soon pass into oblivion; but genius never misses its vocabulary.

A genuine literary artist never uses words which are merely ornamental and therefore extraneous; his phrase contains neither more nor less than his thought; when it fails either by surplusage or by suppression, it falls short of that perfect art which is the instant and final identification of truth and beauty. The artist is known, as Schiller said, by what he omits quite as much as by what he includes. " For in truth all art does but consist in the removal of surplusage, from the last finish of the gem engraver blowing away the last particle of invisible dust, back to the earliest divination of the finished work to be, lying somewhere, according to Michelangelo's fancy, in the rough-hewn block of stone." The artist has no tricks, devices, or artifices ; the secret of his workmanship is not mechanical, but original and vital, and so completely his own that it cannot be detached from him even in thought. When we speak of style in connection with the masters of literary form, — with Shakespeare, with Keats, with Tennyson, with Hawthorne, with Arnold, — we become conscious that we are speaking of something not only obviously beautiful, but mysteriously and inexplicably personal ; something which, although visible and tangible, partakes so largely of the invisible soul that it escapes our analysis. Style is not only the quality which defines a creation as belonging to art, but which, more than any other which we can discover, is most subtly and comprehensively expressive of personality. In it, as in a medium so delicate that it responds to the lightest touch, so stable that it retains the most powerful impression, we discover the compass and resources of a man's soul ; here he reflects himself as in a mirror, not only with conscious purpose, but with that deep unconsciousness the perpetual revelation of which is the deepest inlet of truth into this world of ours.

Dante was the first of the modern poets in time as well as in depth and power; and if we seek for the reason of his primacy in order of literary development, we shall find it in his own work. The poets before him had no clear thought of themselves; they were men not so much of defective as of undeveloped personality. They were bound by traditions, circumscribed by external conditions, ignorant of the authority and the resources of their own souls. They could not trust their intuitions and depend upon their own skill, because they did not know what was within them. They belonged to that dim mediæval world so long under a spell which lulled the personality of men into a deep sleep. That sleep was not without splendid dreams and heavenly visions, but there was no deep and vital sense of reality. Dante was the first to awaken from this sleep. There is no more vigorous personality in history than that of this banished Florentine, who, loving Florence, could live apart from her; saturated with the scholarship of his time, could look upon the world with his own eyes, and substitute his own mother tongue for the conventional Latin; loyal to the Church, could write the doom of popes and priests with unfaltering hand. If one reads carefully, he will find in the " Vita Nuova " the autobiography of the first great modern personality, — the man who turned from the outer to the inner world for truth, who gained complete consciousness of the mighty force within his own nature, and used it with absolute freedom. He was the first poet because he was the first artist; and the secret of his mastery of art lay in the fact that he attained full self-consciousness. For two centuries and a half Italy was crowded with brilliant figures, — men who used all the arts with a freedom and force which have enriched the world for all time. The secret of this protracted and splendid productiveness lies in the tremendous force of personality which was liberated by the Renaissance, — a force which sought expression through every form of creative energy and through every social activity.

In France the same outbreak of personal force appears in the early part of the long reign of Louis XIV.; when the impulse and aspiration of youth and hope were in the air, before prolonged absolutism, exhausting campaigns, and the barrenness of selfish and superficial ideals drained the national life and blighted the national imagination. In the England of Elizabeth there was a liberation of personal force such as no other country has ever seen at a single period. Many of the Elizabethan dramatists impress one as being under a demoniac spell; they are torn and destroyed by their own emotions; a titanic rage possesses them, and, like Marlowe, they push life beyond all bounds in the desperate effort to compass the illimitable and perform the impossible. They fail through excess of force not yet turned into power. They had come to the consciousness of personality, but not to the calmness of self-mastery. Shake-speare came at the very moment when the ferment in the blood was over, and men, no longer blinded by a sudden access of strength, could measure intelligently the force of personality and the strength of the external forces which condition human achievement and expression. Shakespeare had all of Marlowe's force, but he had also clear understanding of the material in which he had to work. He had arrived at full self-knowledge ; and, therefore, of all men of his time, perhaps of all time, his personality had freest and most complete expression. Toward the close of the eighteenth century a similar liberation of personal force was seen in Germany, where a group of great minds appeared, divided by difference of gifts and divergence of situation, but harmonious in this : that each, following boldly the lead of his own genius, discovered the two or three great principles which shape and direct modern thought.

These illustrations will serve to bring out the fact that great literature is possible only when there are great personalities to create it. On the one hand, a great writer puts into his work that which is peculiar to his own nature, and makes it an expression of his deepest and most hidden self; on the other hand, literature depends for its enlargement and expansion on the appearance of men of great and deep personality. Until the idea of personality is developed and becomes general, the creation of literature is impossible. Races which are defective in the sense of personality are incapable of large and varied literary production ; races in which this sense becomes most keen and

general inevitably turn to art. Self-expression is a
necessity when the sense of self becomes deep, rich,
and powerful; when all life awakes to consciousness
through it, and the world lies reflected in it as the
summer night in the sea that moves through it
hushed and calmed as with the deep pulsation of
the universe.

THE SIGNIFICANCE OF MODERN CRITICISM.

IN his essay on "The Study of Poetry," Mr. Arnold warns us against permitting the true estimate of poetry to be superseded by the historical estimate or the personal estimate. The final test of poetry is neither its relation to the development of a nation's language and thought, nor its interest and importance to us by reason of its affinity with our personal tastes and experiences, but the soundness of its substance and perfection of its form. This statement may be so extended in its application as to make it inclusive of all literature. In the nature of things, the highest test can be neither historic nor personal, but must be universal, — a test, that is, which involves primarily truth neither to historic nor to personal relations, but truth to something common to all men in whom the literary instinct has found normal development. When the highest court in Christendom — the consensus of the educated opinion of the world — assigns their relative places to the great writers, this supreme test must always be applied ; but it is only on rare occasions that this supreme tribunal pronounces judgment. Writers of world-wide import, whose work sustains the application of the very highest test, do not come to the judgment-seat of this high tribunal oftener than four or five times in a century. For the most part, it is with the men whose inferiority to Homer and Dante, to Shakespeare and Milton, is clearly apparent that criticism concerns itself. These illustrious shades have received but a single comrade into their immortal fellowship during the present century. Below these foremost names there are written those of a noble company who, if they have failed of the highest places, have come near the shining goal; and it is with these that criticism chiefly concerns itself.

The supreme test separated from all other tests is rarely applied ; the supreme test associated with other and lesser tests is in constant use. Literature is an art, and therefore submits itself to the law of beauty which supplies the test of art ; but it is also a revelation of the spirit of man, and there is to be found in it something more than the perfect felicity and unbroken serenity of the most finely tempered souls. The buoyancy of Homer is one of our great possessions ; but there is something to be learned also from the despondency of Leopardi. The mastery of Shakespeare over all the materials of his work is inspiring ; but there is something significant also in the turbulence of Byron. The amplitude of culture opens the heart of the modern world in Goethe ; but the provincial sincerity of Mistral has something to teach us. Dante's majesty strength makes us feel the identity of great living and great art ; but there is something for us in the pathetic felicity of De Musset and the often unavailing beauty of Shelley. In each writer of any force and genius there is not only the element which makes him amenable to the highest law of criticism, there is also something which appeals to our individual consciousness and is distinctly personal, — something which is the impress of the inheritance and larger circumstance of the time, and is therefore historic, and something which lets us into the soul of a generation of men, or of a period of time or of a deep movement of faith and thought. A great piece of literature may be studied from each of these points of view ; and to get to the bottom of its meaning, it must be so studied. Every enduring literary work not only affords material for, but demands, this comprehensive study, — a study which is at once critical, historic, and personal.

The " Divine Comedy " has been potent enough to give birth to a large literature of secondary and derivative books ; its philosophy, its theology, its cosmology, its politics, its history, its art, have each in turn been subjected to the most searching investigation. We know the rank of the great poem as literature ; we know its historic position in the development of the Italian mind ; we know its profound analysis of the soul and its experiences ; we know what a marvellous revelation of life lies in the heart of it as the supreme and final reward of patient and sympathetic study. No account of Dante's work would be adequate which failed to take into account all these elements of its power. It is something more

than a noble substance of thought encased in a noble
form ; something more than a deep glimpse into experiences which under different names are common to
all men ; something more than a chapter of history
written in fire and blood. It is all these, and it is
something greater. Dante was a man of genius, a
man of wonderful perceptive and receptive power, a
man to feel even more profoundly than he thought,
and to speak even wiser than he knew. Humanity,
under the pressure of that education which we call
history, revealed the unfathomable depth and wonder
of its life through him. We find this same quality of
revelation in Homer, in Shakespeare, in Milton, in
Goethe ; we find it in the work of all men of genius
who have written in prose or verse ; we find it in
Plato, in Marcus Aurelius, in Bacon, in Lessing, in
Carlyle, in Newman, in Emerson. And we find it in
all the great forms which literature takes on, — in
poetry, the drama, fiction, history, essay, criticism.
Every expression of life is not literature ; but nothing
which possesses the indefinable quality of literature
fails to tell us something about that all-embracing
fact. Forms, standards, methods, change ; but the
unchangeable element in all literature is the presence
of some aspect of life reflected, reported, interpreted,
with more or less fidelity and power.

Now, the study of literature in these larger relations, these multiform aspects, has never been so
earnestly pursued as during the present century.
Never before has such a vast amount of material

4

been accumulated; never before have there been such opportunities of using on a great scale the comparative method. This pursuit has become a passion with many of the most sensitive minds ; and we have as a result a body of literary interpre tation and philosophy in the form of criticism so great in mass and so important in substance as to constitute one of the chief distinctively modern contributions to the art of letters. For this study of books and the men who made them is not the pastime of professional Dryasdusts; it is the original and in a large measure the creative work of those who, in other literary periods and under other intellectual and social influences, would have illustrated their genius through the epic, the drama, or the lyric. Lessing, Herder, Goethe, Coleridge, Carlyle, Sainte-Beuve, Arnold, Amiel, Emerson, Lowell, and Stedman have not been students of the work of other men simply from force of the scholarly impulse; they have been irresistibly attracted to the study of literature because literature has disclosed to them the soul and the laws of life and art. The passion for contact with the great and inexhaustible impulses which unify human life under all conditions has led these diligent explorers from one continent to another until a new world lies within our ken. Each literature in turn is yielding its secrets of race inheritance, temperament, genius; each related group of literatures is disclosing the common characteristics of the family of races behind it ; each literary epoch is revealing the spiritual, moral, and social forces which dominated it; each great literary form is discovering its intimate and necessary relation with some fact of life, some stage or process of experience. We know the Greek race in large measure through the Greek literature; we know the unspent forces which stirred the Elizabethan age through the Elizabethan writers; and we know why, at intervals, the greatest literary minds have used the drama, the lyric, the novel, as forms of expression. All this we owe to the modern critical movement, — a movement not so much of study and comparison for the purposes of judgment by fixed standards, as of investigation for the purpose of laying bare the common laws of life and art; of making it clear to us that literature is always the vital utterance of insight and experience.

The earliest development of criticism on any considerable scale — the criticism of Alexandria and of the later stages of the revival of classical learning in Italy, for example — was largely textual; it concerned itself chiefly with the settlement of questions of variant versions; it was mainly and necessarily absorbed in a study of words and phrases. Criticism of the higher order — criticism which searches for the laws of beauty in the creations of art — is not possible until there has been a large accumulation of material upon which it can work. The drama must pass through the entire period of its development, from its rudimentary form in the chorus to its perfection in the plays of Sophocles, before Aristotle announces its laws and defines its aims. Not until a literary form has been completely worked out does it disclose the law of its interior structure and its resources of expression. Nor can any single work of literary art furnish the elements for æsthetic criticism ; there must be kindred works with which comparison may be made and resemblances or contrasts noted. When æsthetic criticism is fully equipped and developed, there remains still another stage in the evolution ; the criticism which deals with literature as a whole, which studies the large conditions under which it is created, which takes account of race, time, circumstance, which discerns in the detached works of a man or a generation or race an adequate expression of human experience and an authentic revelation of human life, is still to come ; and this larger criticism is not possible until universal literature is open to the critic. It is true that these different and progressive stages are not always clearly defined ; they shade into each other, as do the various forms of animal and vegetable life. They are often contemporaneous in the same piece of critical work ; comment on questions of text, illustration of æsthetic quality, and recognition of rank and significance in the general movement of history often go hand in hand in the work of a critic of the first rank. Nevertheless, these three stages of the development of criticism are distinctly and unmistakably marked.

Textual criticism may begin with the first study of a literary work, since it concerns that work alone,

and has no relation to literature at large. Textual
criticism of the Iliad and Odyssey began, doubtless,
with the attempt, in the time of Pisistratus, to collect
these wandering stories. Æsthetic criticism was
only possible when the beauty and truth of these
great works had so penetrated and enlightened the
Greek mind that soundness of substance and perfection of form were recognized as the tests of a
genuine work of art. The laws of art have always
been discovered by the process of induction ; no race
has ever thought much about art in the abstract
until it has been educated by contact with works
which, by their revelation to the eye, have made the
mind conscious of its own affinity with the ideals of
beauty. The discovery of the same laws in the works
of literature has followed a similar order. The lyric
must sing in the hearts of men before the secret of
its form is discerned and disclosed ; the drama must
unfold the iron creed of fate, or the indissoluble
union of character and destiny, before the laws
which shape it are announced. Æsthetic criticism
follows, therefore, those productive periods which, by
enlargement and enrichment of the scope of actual
achievement, disclose new sources of power, larger
sweep of ideas, different or higher possibilities of
execution. When Euripides completed his work, the
Greek had all the materials for an intelligent, if still
incomplete, study of the drama at hand ; Æschylus,
Sophocles, and Euripides had wrought with such
power on so great a scale that they had made clear

the construction and the peculiar force and significance of the noble literary form which they fashioned.
There was no need, for the purposes of æsthetic
criticism, to hold judgment in suspense until Lessing,
Corneille, Calderon, and Shakespeare had spoken.
Aristotle was amply justified by the scope and
splendour of the drama of his own race in declaring
the purpose of all dramatic representation. But as a
disclosure of the full possibilities of the drama as an
instrument of human expression, even the Attic stage
was incomplete ; other races must endure and suffer
and translate experience into art, before the full compass of this magnificent literary form could be understood. And when the drama has been brought as
near perfection as the genius of man can carry it,
there are still other elements which must enter into a
final and adequate comprehension of its significance.
It must be studied in the light of a complete literary
development ; it must find its place in the large
movement of history. To a real mastery of the
drama as a form of art and an expression of experience, there is necessary, therefore, its full development
under many diverse conditions and at many hands,
familiarity with literature in all its forms, and clear
perception of the historic life behind the work of art.
And what is true of the drama is also true of the epic,
the lyric, the ballad, the novel, — in a word, of
literature as a whole.

The conditions which make possible this comprehensive study of literature as an art, and as an

expression of human life, have not existed until within comparatively recent times. There are glimpses here and there in the works of the greatest minds of the unity of knowledge, glimpses of the range and significance of literature as the vital outcome of all human experience ; but the clear perception of these truths has been possible only to modern men. It is one thing to glance at a great truth in the swift vision of prophecy ; it is a very different thing to discern it as the result of deliberate searching, and to hold it within the field until it is clearly understood in its import and large relations. So long as knowledge and art were abstractly conceived, — thought of as existing apart and isolated from human development, — there could be no conception of their harmony and interdependence, of their vital relation to the development of men as individuals and as a society. It was reserved for the Germans of the last century to comprehend and formulate that idea of the unity and vital interdependence of all the forms and forces of civilization which lies at the foundation of all our modern thinking; which has, indeed, transformed and reconstructed all knowledge.

What the Humanists did in a partial and provisional way toward a true and real insight into the antique world, the great German critics of the last century — Winckelmann, Herder, Lessing, and Goethe — did fundamentally and permanently, not only for classical art and life, but for all knowledge and history. The Humanists destroyed the mediæval tradition of Virgil, and brought back the living man; brushed aside the cobwebs with which centuries of monkish teaching had obscured the great poem, and made clear once more its human tenderness and beauty. The German thinkers destroyed the abstract idea of knowledge which divided it into separate departments, isolated from each other and detached from the living experience of men, — the formal, academic idea of art as a set of rules, a fixed and conventional practice unrelated to national character. Rejecting the dry and arbitrary definitions and abstractions of his time, Winckelmann discovered the totality of Greek life, and saw what his predecessors had failed to see, — that simplicity, elevation, and repose were the common qualities of the dramas of Sophocles, the marbles of Phidias, the speculations of Plato, the orations of Pericles; that literature, sculpture, philosophy, and oratory were, therefore, the vitally related parts of a harmonious and complete expression of Greek life; and that the common root whence all these exquisite flowers drew their loveliness was the Greek nature. Many of the marbles in the Vatican were recovered as part of the great work of the Renaissance, but they were first really seen by Winckelmann and his contemporaries. He discerned the noble idealism shared alike by Plato and the sculptors of the Periclean age, — that idealism which found in the Greek mind so congenial a soil, and in the Greek hand and the Greek speech such sure and marvellous interpreters. Winckelmann

" first unveiled the ideal beauty of Greek antiquity,"
and disclosed those qualities of Greek art which make
it one in all its splendid forms; so that whether we
study the trilogy of Agamemnon, the structure of the
Parthenon, the statesmanship of Pericles, or the
" Phædrus," we are conscious of but a single creative
personality. In its magical beauty each work remains a perpetual type ; but the genius of the lamp
by which these wonders were wrought was one. Behind all these beautiful masks there was a single
face. Winckelmann saw that art had a natural history
of its own, and that its birth, its successive stages of
growth, its decay and death, could be clearly traced ;
he saw that religion, political development, race,
climate, soil, character, furnished the conditions of
its life. He perceived, in a word, the unity of Greek
life and history, the organic and historic development
of Greek art. For an abstract idea, he substituted
a living organism ; for a conventional system, a vital
process ; for an isolated skill, the splendid expression
of the deepest human experience and the loftiest
human ideals.

By very different methods, and with a very different
mind, but in the same vital spirit, Herder approached
the study of literature. French influence was still
dominant in Germany, where the absolutism of Frederick in the State was reproduced in letters in the
tyranny of artificial tastes, conventional models, and
a dead formality alien to the German mind and
powerless to touch the German heart. Boileau's

" Art Poétique " was the final word concerning literature ; while the sovereignty of fact and the supremacy
of common-sense, incarnated in the " Encyclopædia,"
barred out the visions of the imagination and the
insight of intuition.   In this formal world, from which
all natural, primary impulses were shut out, Herder
appeared, fresh from contact with the living sources of
literature.   He was saturated with the poetry of the
Bible ; he had drunk deep at the springs of Homer,
Shakespeare, and the English ballads.   He was under
the spell of the freshest and most creative spirit ever
expressed in literature, — a spirit instinctively artistic in
every expression of itself, and yet without a touch of
self-consciousness.   Nowhere has the soul of man
spoken with such perfect simplicity and sincerity,
and consequently with such sublime eloquence, as in
the pages of the Bible, of Homer, and of Shakespeare.
Herder exchanged the old-fashioned French garden,
with its deformed trees and intrusive orderliness, for
the bloom of the open field.   Literature was no artificial product to him ; it was a natural growth ; its
roots were in the heart of man ; it was the voice of
man's need and sufferings and hopes.   From the
conventional ideas and standards of his time he
turned to the profound conception of literature as a
growth, an unforced and authoritative utterance of
the soul.   He returned to Nature, in the well-worn
phrase ; to Nature as he found it in primitive ages,
and in men whose simplicity and sincerity were still
untouched by conventionalism.   " Poetry in those

happy days," he declared, " lived in the ears of the
people, on the lips and in the harps of living bards ;
it sang of history, of the events of the day, of mysteries, miracles, and signs. It was the flower of a
nation's character, language, and country, of its occupations, its prejudices, its passions, its aspirations,
and its soul." The epic was to Herder " the living
history of the people ; " the *Lied*, or song, was not a
poem of the study and the salon ; it was a natural
melody out of the heart of a passion or sentiment.
The fable was not a calculated setting of moral truth
in story form ; it was " the poetical illustration of a
lesson of experience by means of a characteristic
trait, drawn from animal life, and developed by analogy." " Analogy is the parent of poetry in fables,
not abstraction, still less a dry deduction from the
general to the particular." Herder opposed to the
mechanical conception of literature, then almost universally held, the vital conception ; he recognized
the distinctive quality of genius, because he emphasized the spontaneous element in all great poetry ;
he discerned the parallelism between literary and
historical development. The significant word with
him was growth ; because growth implies natural
process as opposed to mechanical process, spontaneous impulse as opposed to conscious action, genius
as opposed to artifice, the individual soul as opposed
to abstract ideas. Goethe expressed Herder's fundamental idea when he said : " Everything that man
undertakes to produce, whether by action, word, or

in whatsoever way, ought to spring from the union of all his faculties." It is this deep, unconscious expression of the totality of man's experience and nature which pervades the greatest works of literature, and makes them the most authoritative works of history we possess. They record the progress of that education of the soul for which the world stands.

Herder performed for literature the service which Winckelmann performed for antique art : he discovered its natural history, and set it in normal relations with the totality of human thought and achievement. And what he had done for literature he did also for history. He substituted a natural and vital for an artificial and mechanical conception. He grasped the great idea of development, so familiar to us, and so fruitful of fresher and deeper views of things. "Up to this time," says a German writer, reported by Hillebrand, from whom these quotations are made, "the most mechanical teleology had reigned in the philosophy of history. Providence was represented to have created cork-trees that men should have wherewith to stop their bottles." Herder saw that the laws which govern the life of men in the world are written in the very constitution of the soul, and are not arbitrary regulations impressed from without; that history records the unfolding of germs and forces which were within the soul at the beginning, not a series of interferences and interruptions; and that these germs are developed under conditions fixed by law, and part, therefore, of the very structure of Nature. "The God I look for in history," he said, "must be the same as the God of Nature, — for man is but a tiny particle of the whole, and the history of mankind resembles that of the worm, closely connected with the tissue it inhabits; therefore the natural laws by which the Deity reveals itself must reign in man likewise. . . . The whole history of humanity is pure, natural history of human forces, actions, and instincts, according to time and place." If Herder meant in these words to shut out the constant inflow of spiritual influences into human history, we might well part company with him; but the emphasis of his statement and its deep significance are to be found in the fact that he vitalized history as he had vitalized literature, by putting a natural process of growth in the place of a mechanical process, thus making history a living expression of the character of man, — a continuous revelation of the laws and forces of life.

Those only who understand how widespread and deep-rooted were mechanical and arbitrary ideas in the last century can understand how tremendous a revolution was implicit in the changes of thought thus rapidly sketched, — a revolution which has affected every department of knowledge, and has reorganized it along new and deeper lines. Carlyle once said to Bayard Taylor that Goethe had been his saviour. There was a characteristic exaggeration in the statement; but it had this truth at the bottom, that at a time when the young Scotch thinker found himself

forced to part company with the narrow and arid
conception of life and humanity as vitiated by
corruption, and not only entirely untrustworthy, but
dissevered and broken into fragments, the buoyant
naturalism of Goethe, affirming the divine origin
and destiny of all created things, the soundness and
healthfulness of Nature and man, the unity and
dignity of history and knowledge, and consequently
the authority of history, literature, and art as a
revelation of both human and divine, put solid ground
under him, and gave him a rational and harmonious
view of things, — a view which included and made
room for every form of human activity. It is very
interesting to the reader of Goethe to-day to discover
how generally the intellectual movement of this
century is reflected in his pages, and how profoundly
sympathetic his mind was with the broad and, within
certain limits, healthy and fruitful naturalism which
pervades contemporary thought. The nature of man
was to Goethe the one authoritative and authentic
revelation, and he refused to reject any part of that
revelation. History, literature, art, religion, — these
all expressed what man has been and has become by
virtue of the evolution of his personality under the
established conditions of life. The natural history of
man is written in his works, and together they form
the trustworthy record and disclosure of his nature.

It will be seen from this brief statement that
Winckelmann, Herder, and Goethe held certain fundamental ideas in common, and these ideas will be

found to be fundamental in modern criticism. The perception of the truth that literature is, in large measure, conditioned on the development, the surroundings, and the character of the men who create it; that the vast and varied movement of humanity recorded in history is a development, a progressive unfolding, a coherent expression of man's nature; and that literature, as a part of this vast movement, represents a growth, a vital process, and is, therefore, a part of the discovery of himself which man is making as his supreme achievement in life, — these are the informing ideas of the modern critical movement. The epoch of purely textual criticism has long passed away; that work has been transferred mainly, if not entirely, to the scholars. Æsthetic criticism, on the other hand, has been immensely enriched and stimulated by the application to literature of the ideas which have been set forth; never in the history of letters has there been so much criticism of the highest order as during the present century. When it was seen that no literary work is detached from the totality of human achievement; that no work represents individual gift, skill, or experience alone; that in every real book humanity speaks out of and to its own heart, — the feeling toward literature was immensely deepened and freshened. Æsthetic criticism formerly concerned itself entirely with the fidelity of a work to standards already set up by the creations of acknowledged masters; this was the kind of criticism which was practised in England and on the continent at the close of the last and the beginning of the present century. It was assumed that the last word had been spoken concerning the art of writing; that the final canons had been announced, and the final standards and models given to the world. A new work must conform to these standards or suffer condemnation; lack of conformity meant lack of art. Now, the very idea of literature as a growth, as an expression of the continually unfolding life of man, involves not only the possibility, but the certainty, of change and expansion. New forms of expression must be born with the new thoughts and experiences which they are to clothe. The permanent element in literature is not form, but spirit; not a particular manner, but perfection of manner; not uniformity of execution, but endless variety, stamped always with supreme excellence. There are flawless models, but they are for inspiration, not for imitation; they fix the standard of quality, but they liberate the hand which they inspire.

This was perhaps the first great change effected by the modern way of looking at literature; and the extent and significance of that change can be seen by comparing the criticism of Voltaire with that of Sainte-Beuve; the criticism of Dr. Johnson with that of Matthew Arnold. The older view of literature involved the idea of a fixed and formal set of laws constituting an art; the later view involves the growth of literature with the growth of man, the essential element being, not conformity to a rigid order of form, but soundness and veracity of thought, and beauty and flexibility of expression. Dr. Johnson could understand Dryden because Dryden was a conformist, in letter if not in spirit; but Shakespeare belonged to another order, and demanded a breadth and catholicity which Dr. Johnson could not bring to his magical pages. Mr. Arnold, on the other hand, can perceive the literary quality shared in common by men as diverse as Wordsworth and Shelley, as Byron and Tolstoi. The criticism represented by Mr. Arnold, even when it limits itself to æsthetic quality alone, is informed with modern ideas; with the ideas which Herder and his contemporaries were the first to see clearly and to apply profoundly. No man studies a star as a solitary world; though he shut all other stars out of the field of observation, the heavens still move about the shining point which he has isolated. A modern critic approaches a work of literature with certain ideas which are a part of his intellectual life. He cannot, if he would, detach a writer from his age, his race, humanity: all these are present in every study which he makes; they are involved in every conclusion which he reaches; they contribute to every judgment which he pronounces.

The older criticism, the criticism based on standards which were supposed to be exact and final, must in the nature of things have continued to be a derivative and secondary growth, —a body of writing related to the original work of which it treated, very much as the parasite is related to the trunk from

5

which it draws its life. But for the development of
the ideas which have been emphasized, criticism as
we know it could never have been. For when we
study this criticism as a whole, we become aware
that it is original and not secondary work; and that
criticism as a literary form has as deep a root, and
is as clearly related to human growth and experience
as the epic, the drama, or any other form of distinctively creative work. The extent to which this form
has been used by men of literary genius of late years,
and the perfection to which it has been brought, indicate clearly that there is behind it a primary impulse, — an impulse which seeks it as something
normal, adequate, and akin to the spirit and thought
of the day. It is sometimes said that the great place
in contemporary literature occupied by criticism is
evidence of the decline of the creative impulse, and
that the originative forces are evidently spent. This
class of comment is familiar to all students of literature, who have read again and again the announce-
ment of a similar decay of art because some new form
of expression had begun to press hard upon the old
in importance and influence. The literary instinct,
like every kind of artistic instinct, is characterized by
the greatest sensitivism; men select forms of expression rarely as the result of deliberation; the form
comes generally with the message which it is to contain, or the significant fact which it is to express. If
a literary form attracts a great number of fine minds
at a given time, this fact of itself raises the presump-

tion that the attractive power lies in some deep and real affinity between this particular form and the intellectual and spiritual conditions of the time. Without consideration of the contents of modern criticism, the fact that so many minds of the highest class have made it their chief means of self-expression ought to put us on guard against any conclusion involving its rank as an original contribution to literature. That men of the order of Coleridge, Carlyle, Sainte-Beuve, and Arnold have chosen criticism as the method of expression best fitted to convey their convictions and conclusions is a sufficient answer to those who regard it as a secondary form, and refuse to recognize it as original and first-hand work. Not exhaustion of creative impulse, but change of direction, is indicated by the attractiveness of criticism to modern minds; not a decline of force, but the application of force through a new instrument.

The scientific spirit has invaded literature to the extent of emphasizing the importance of a clear comprehension of all the elements that enter into a work of literary art so far as they are discoverable. The secret of the splendid vitality of the Odyssey eludes all search; but we recognize it the more clearly now that we have learned so much about the Greek life and character out of which it issued and in which it was embosomed. But this spirit, in its devotion to reality and its instinct for getting to the bottom of things, could not rest in any isolated study of literary works; it must study literature as a whole, determine its rank and place, and interpret its significance in the totality of human development. It is in the body of modern critical writing that we discover the response of the literary mind to the methods and spirit of science. The absorbing search of science is for the fact, and the law behind the fact; it fashions nothing; it waits with infinite patience on discovery. Now, the end of criticism is, to this extent, identical with the end of science; it is to discover and lay bare the fact, and the law behind it. Is this work true to the fact, the law? is its first question; and the answer involves a clear discernment of the truth of idea or experience which the writer has sought to represent under the form of art, and also a clear perception of the law of beauty to which it must conform if it contain the indefinable quality of art. Thus, as its most immediate and direct result, criticism discovers the presence or absence of soundness of substance and perfection of form.

But there is another and more comprehensive question which criticism asks. The work which it studies must conform to something, but it must also reveal something; it must disclose a certain order and beauty of workmanship, but it must also discover its connection with an ultimate order to which every real expression of man's soul bears witness. When Matthew Arnold defines poetry as a criticism of life, he indicates that which is behind all literature, whether in verse or prose, — that which supplies its inspiration and furnishes its unfailing test. What is soundness of substance but fidelity to the fact and law of life? A work of art is sound only when it is true to nature and experience ; it may possess the very highest beauty, but if, like some of Shelley's longer poems, it lacks reality, truth to experience or to ideals which are the projection of experience, we are compelled to assign it a lower rank. It is defective in that quality which is, so far as substance is concerned, the supreme quality of the really great work of art. And what is perfection of form but fidelity to those laws of art never put on tables of stone, but indelibly written in the soul by the hand whose vast creation follows ever the line of beauty? The fact and the law of life and art, — these are the realities for which criticism, consciously or unconsciously, is always searching. These form what Fichte called "the divine idea of the world," which "lies at the bottom of all appearance." Herder, Goethe, Hildebrand, and Grimm ; Sainte-Beuve and Scherer; Coleridge, Carlyle, Arnold, Dowden, and Hutton ; Emerson and Lowell, — the great company of those who have pursued criticism for the highest ends have each and all disclosed the power of these ideas upon their work. They have fashioned a new form of literature, and one perfectly adapted to the intellectual methods and tendencies of the age, — a form through which the creative impulse, following the scientific method, but in the truest literary spirit, works with a freedom and power which attest the adaptation of the instrument to the task. Perfection of form is nowhere more perfectly illustrated than in the best critical writing, in which the more imposing qualities of order, proportion, gradation, are combined with marvellous delicacy of touch, refinement of characterization, subtilty and keenness of insight.

Modern criticism has given us a new conception of literature. Studying comprehensively the vast material which has come to its hand, discerning clearly the law of growth behind all art, and the interdependence and unity of all human development, it has given us an interpretation of literature which is nothing less than another chapter in the revelation of life. This is its real contribution to civilization ; this is the achievement which stamps it as creative work. The epic described adequately and nobly the stir and movement of an objective age ; the drama represented the relations of men to the powers above them and to the organized social and moral forces about them ; criticism, in the hands of the great writers, discloses the law and the fact of art and life as these final realities are revealed through literature.

THE POETRY OF DANTE GABRIEL ROSSETTI.

THE real importance of those movements in literature or art which have been definite enough in aim
to enlist an active membership of gifted persons
and to formulate something like a creed, is to be
found, as a rule, not in the creed, but in the fellowship. The formulation of principles, the agreement
upon methods, seem at the moment of the first importance ; but time, that patient corrector of inadequate judgments and false perspectives, is indifferent
to theories of art, and cares only for the work which
discovers the inspired touch, and the personality
through which the vision of truth or beauty enters
into the common life of men. Such movements are
often fruitful of great works and great souls, and
mark great expansions of thought ; but the specific
creeds which they profess, like creeds of every sort,
are always partial, inadequate, and provisional. That
which seemed a finality to the men who were under
the spell of its fresh and thrilling influence, in the
end falls into line with the continuous process of
development of which it was part, and is recognized
as a new and fruitful evolution from the past.

To the ardent youths who crowded the Théâtre Français on the evening of Feb. 25, 1830, "Hernani" filled the entire stage of the world and obliterated the drama of the past; in that hour Romanticism was not so much a reaction as a complete and final revolution of the aims and principles of dramatic art. To many of the Transcendentalists of forty years ago the pure and highly intellectual impulse which they shared prophesied the breaking of the last seals, and the imminent disclosure of that open secret which has been in all times both inspiration and anguish to the noblest souls. No student of literature will underestimate the value of those statements of principles, vague and incomplete as they were, which grew out of the Romantic and Transcendental movements; but the real significance of Romanticism and Transcendentalism is to be found in the substantial works which attest to the world the reality of the impulse which inspired them, and in which the main drift of both movements is to be discovered. Much has been written concerning Pre-Raphaelitism, and much doubtless remains to be said touching this very interesting movement which affected English art so strongly forty years ago; but the significance and value of the impulse which strove with only partial success to formulate itself in the "Germ" and, later, in the "Oxford and Cambridge Magazine," is to be found in the works of three or four eminent artists, and of at least one poet of rare quality and unique personality. We are chiefly concerned to know that the Pre-Raphaelite movement, like every other great movement in art and literature, was not so much the outcome of a new doctrine, a novel creed, as a new attitude toward Nature and life, a more sincere and earnest mood, a fresh perception of truth and beauty through individual genius, a deep and spontaneous feeling for things which had come to be treated in a conventional and formal way. The significance of such movements lies always in the fact that they mark fresh contact of open and aspiring minds with Nature and life ; and when this takes place, ferment, agitation, and brilliant activity inevitably follow. The artists and poets who are associated with Pre-Raphaelitism were moved by a common instinct to forsake the conventional and academic methods of the day and study Nature for themselves ; this was the wholesome impulse at the heart of their common activity, and its sincerity and power are the more apparent now that the excessive individualism and morbid intensity of much of its expression have become things of the past.

It would be interesting as matter of literary history to indicate the relations of this movement to the larger movement of thought and life which set its impress on the literature of Europe at the close of the last and the beginning of the present century. Herder and the young Goethe ; Burns, Byron, Keats, Shelley, Coleridge, and Wordsworth ; Hugo and Gautier, — are names which seem to suggest differences rather than agreement ; but it would not be difficult

to discover certain near and close ties between them.
More evident and readily discoverable is the relationship of Pre-Raphaelitism with Romanticism ; with the
Oxford movement which expressed itself from the
pulpit of St. Mary's Church in those subtile and
searching sermons which made the world aware that
in John Henry Newman a man of distinctly religious
genius had appeared ; and with that notable revival
of Gothic forms which a deepened religious feeling
substituted for the pseudo-classic architecture of the
preceding century. A wonderfully interesting and
significant movement of thought and life was that
which associated the names of Newman and Keble,
Hunt, Millais, and Rossetti, Pugin and Ruskin. But
this is, after all, mainly matter of historical interest ;
the real message which these men had to deliver to
the world is to be sought not so much in their statements of faith, which were largely polemic, as in the
great works which are the only authentic disclosures
of their genius and bent. The men themselves had
no sooner come to agreement in certain specific
matters of principle or method than they began immediately to drift apart ; the law of life was upon
them ; and while they held some things in common,
the work and the word of each was to be the utterance of individual insight and experience.

Of the seven young men who formed the Pre-
Raphaelite Brotherhood in 1848, William Holman
Hunt, John Everett Millais, and Dante Gabriel
Rossetti achieved distinction as painters ; Thomas

Woolner as a sculptor; William M. Rossetti and his famous brother, as poets; while James Collinson and Frederick George Stephens, either in promise or performance, made good their claim to this illustrious companionship. With these names are also associated others which the world will not care to forget: Madox Brown, the painter of the Manchester frescos, William Bell Scott, and Christina Rossetti. To this little group the Rossetti family furnished three of the most active and original minds; and of these three, one is likely to remain the most memorable exponent of the Pre-Raphaelite movement. Of Gabriel Charles Dante Rossetti, who changed his name to Dante Gabriel at an early period in his career, much might be said by way of emphasizing the influential element of heredity. In blood, as his brother tells us, he was three fourths Italian and one fourth English, " being on the father's side wholly Italian and on the mother's side half Italian and half English." The father was a scholar, a man of letters, and an ardent patriot long before the days of the successful movement for Italian independence and nationality. Exiled after the good old Bourbon fashion, Gabriele Rossetti came to London in 1824, married the daughter of an English mother and an Italian father, — the latter a teacher, translator, and scholar of excellent quality, — became Professor of Italian in King's College, and a commentator on Dante of orthodox depth and obscurity. To this fugitive scholar were born four children, — Maria Francesca, who died in 1876;

Dante Gabriel; William Michael; and Christina Georgina. A group so variously gifted has rarely gathered round any fireside. To Maria Francesca we are indebted for " A Shadow of Dante," which so eminent a student of the great Florentine as Mr. Lowell has declared to be " by far the best comment that has appeared in English." William Michael is known to all readers of current English verse and criticism; and Christina has won high rank as a writer of lyrical verse of marked individual quality.

Dante Gabriel was born on May 12, 1828, into an atmosphere charged with high and intense intellectual activity. He knew the story of " Hamlet " before most children know the alphabet, and at five years of age he wrote a dramatic poem entitled " The Slave ; " seven years later he composed a series of still more ambitious verses which bore the romantic title of " Sir Hugh the Heron," and were probably suggested by some lines in the first canto of " Marmion." These verses have no interest save as they indicate the precocious activity of a mind which began its conscious development with the advantages of an exceptional pre-natal education. In 1835 he entered King's College school, where he studied Latin, French, and German ; Italian was as familiar to him as English. A strong desire to become a painter led to a change of instruction in his fourteenth year ; and leaving King's College school, he devoted himself to the study of art. From the Royal Academy Antique School he entered the studio of Madox Brown, and

o

made the acquaintance of the daring young innovators who formed the Pre-Raphaelite Brotherhood in 1848. In his nineteenth year Dante Gabriel wrote the first verse which gave unmistakable evidence of his possession of poetic genius. In this year he produced the striking lines entitled " My Sister's Sleep," in the metre with which " In Memoriam " was to make the world familiar three years later; and the most widely known of all his poems, " The Blessed Damosel ; " both of which appeared for the first time in the " Germ " in 1850. Of Rossetti's art work, begun at this period and carried on to the close of his too brief career, this is not the place to speak, even if it were within the power of the writer to characterize and describe its subtile and varied beauty of expression, its noble substance of thought, its splendour and depth of imaginative force. It is sufficient to say that the two sides of his life endeavour are entirely harmonious ; that they are complementary expressions of a genius which saw things as a whole with a glance that pierced to the very soul of beauty in things visible and in a vision as rapt and at times as ecstatic as was ever vouchsafed to mystic or saint.

In the spring of 1860, after a long engagement, Rossetti married Elizabeth Eleanor Siddal, — a woman of poetic and artistic faculty, of exquisite sensitiveness of mind and nature, and whose beautiful face will long remain a possession in one of Rossetti's most characteristic works, the " Beata Beatrix." The completeness and happiness of this fellowship can only be inferred from the crushing and lifelong grief which her death, early in 1862, brought upon Rossetti. In the darkness of that sudden and awful sorrow, to quote the words of another, the poet literally buried his wand, and committed his poems to the grave in which his wife was interred. But neither genius nor its works are private property, and the time came when the persuasions of his friends and his own sense of obligation to his gifts induced Rossetti to consent to the disinterment of the manuscripts; and in 1876 his first volume of "Poems" was published, — the second volume, "Ballads and Sonnets," appearing in 1881. But the hand of death was already upon him. Insomnia, that lurking foe in sensitive and highly imaginative temperaments, had already greatly reduced his working power, and had developed a morbid tendency which led to recurring periods of depression and to prolonged seclusion from the society of all save the most intimate friends. On Easter Sunday, April 9, 1882, Rossetti died.

A singularly uneventful life, judged by that shallowest of conventional standards which measures the depth and breadth of man's life by the journeys he makes, and the things which befall his estate! Rossetti's life was intensive rather than extensive; its power and affluence lay in the clearness with which its own aims were discerned, and the quiet persistence with which it was held to the lines of its own development. Probably no modern man has been, in one sense, so detached from the world of his time, and so consistently true to an ideal which was the projection of his own soul. That ideal is clearly disclosed in the two arts which served Rossetti as interpreters with almost equal fidelity and power. No man has left a more distinct record of his temperament and genius, and there are few such records which put one under a spell more potent, or which lead one on to the heart of a more enthralling ideal. A man so sensitive and intense in his imaginative faculty will not fall under the influence of a multitude of antagonistic teachers; he will respond only to those with whom his own nature has some spiritual kinship. One is not surprised to find, therefore, that Rossetti early discovered strongly marked intellectual affinities, which lie so directly along the lines of his own temperament that, after studying his work, one could safely venture to name them. Shakespeare, Byron, Shelley, Coleridge, Keats, and Tennyson are the natural teachers of such a boyhood and youth as Rossetti's; and later one may count with assurance upon the peculiar and potent influence of Blake and Browning. There is one other name with which the name of Rossetti will be associated as long as it carries any power of association with it. Over the household of the exiled Italian scholar the memory of Dante continually hovered like the presence of the genius of a race. The great Florentine was not a tradition, the shadow of a mighty past, to the childhood of the poet; he was a continual and pervasive influence, penetrating his inmost life in its formative period, and leaving in the mind an image as clear and familiar as it was inspiring. Rossetti's personality was too strong and well defined to yield itself even into hands so puissant as those of Dante; but between the two there was a spiritual as well as a race kinship, and the poet of the "Divine Comedy" has had no truer interpreter than the translator of the "Vita Nuova" and the poet of "The House of Life."

Rossetti was extremely fond of the old English and Scotch ballad literature. For the Italian poets as a whole he cared little; among modern writers of French verse he was drawn only to Hugo and De Musset; his admiration for Villon one could safely have predicted. He had little in common with the Germans, whose names were on all lips in the time of his early manhood, although one cannot help thinking that if he had carried his study of the language further, he would have been strongly moved by many of the German ballads, and that at least one episode in "Faust" would have touched him closely. Fitzgerald's masterly version of Calderon interested him greatly during the later years of his life. For Teutonic and Scandinavian myth and poetry he had no affinity, and he was entirely free from that curiosity concerning Oriental thought and belief which of late has taken possession of so many minds, both great and small. He had none of that unfruitful and essentially unintellectual curiosity which leads people to ransack all literatures and philosophies, not in the spirit of eager search for principles, but from a desire to discover some new thing, — a desire especially to come upon some esoteric knowledge, and thus, by a single brilliant advance, possess themselves of the secret of the universe. Rossetti did not make the mistake of thinking that truth is something which can be found by searching; he understood that knowledge becomes truth only as we grow into it and make it ours by vital assimilation. Deaf to all solicitations of passion or pleasure, unresponsive to the intellectual curiosity of his time, he took his own way through life, made fellowship with those who shared with him the passion for the ideal, and gave his work the impress of a singular and highly individual consistency of conception and mood.

Two volumes of moderate size contain the complete work of Rossetti in poetry, and one of these is made up of translations. It is the quality rather than the quantity of the work which gives it claim to consideration. We could ill afford to lose any of the Shakespearian dramas or of the longer poems of Tennyson or Browning; these poets survey and interpret so wide a field of thought that the complete expression of the genius of either would suffer mutilation by suppression or loss. But Rossetti was not in touch with the wide movement of life; he was absorbed in a single pursuit, and enthralled by a single ideal; within comparatively narrow limits he has given us a complete picture of the vision that was reflected in the depths of his soul. The volume of translations, "Dante and His Circle," attests not only his great familiarity with

6

the early Italian poets, but also his extraordinary mastery of difficult metrical forms. In his own verse Rossetti used few forms, but they were among the most expressive and exacting; in his translations he showed himself master of the principles of an art to the practice of which the early Italians brought all their characteristic subtilty and refinement. This volume discloses something more than the possession of those gifts which go to the making of a genuine translation; it discloses a genius for poetry of a very high order. No one but a poet worthy of Dante's companionship could have entered so completely into the purpose of the "Vita Nuova," and disposed about the great Florentine in such effective and luminous grouping the company of singers who preceded, accompanied, or immediately followed, the master. The sonnets, canzonets, and lyrics, which represent the work of more than forty different writers, are rendered into English with a fidelity of spirit, beauty of form, and melody of phrase which betray Rossetti's double mastery of Italian thought and English speech.

When we turn to his own work, we find the subtilty and delicacy of the Italian genius still present, but new and personal qualities appear to attest the possession of original gifts as well as of inherited aptitudes. It was chiefly through the ballad, the lyric, and the sonnet that Rossetti spoke to the world; and although in the use of each of these forms he showed at times a high degree of metrical

skill, it will probably appear in the end that his genius
had more kinship with the sonnet than with either
lyric or ballad, and that among all his contemporaries
his mastery of this delicate instrument which the
Italians formed was most complete. It is not easy,
however, to discriminate between varieties of form in
a mass of work so full of deep poetic emotion and
thought as Rossetti's. His ballads grow in beauty
and power as we penetrate more and more their often
obscure meaning. It is not alone their quaint
phraseology, their archaic turns of speech, their
recurring use of obsolete but picturesque words, that
impress us with a sense of something not akin to our
thought or time ; it is the mediæval spirit which
pervades them and gives them a deep and moving
spell, a glow and splendour such as shine through
cloister windows when vesper chants are sung. The
ballad as a literary form belongs to social and intellectual conditions which have passed away never to
return ; but it still offers to a genius like Rossetti's
resources of expression not to be found in any other
form of verse. It is so nearly akin to the lyric that
it brings the rhythmical movement and thrill of the
singing note to the narration of objective events and
actions ; and it is so full of dramatic resources that it
adds to directness of expression the varied and contrasted motives of the drama. It combines lyrical
music with dramatic intensity and cumulative force.
The seven ballads which Rossetti wrote illustrate the
power and beauty with which a poet of genius can

inspire a form of verse which has ceased in a sense
to be a natural note for modern thought. "Stratton
Water," "The White Ship," and "The King's
Tragedy" approach very nearly the romantic and
historic type of the true ballad, and are thoroughly
dramatic in spirit, although charged with intense
individualism; "Troy Town," "Eden Bower,"
"Rose Mary," and "Sister Helen" belong to the
world of imaginative creation, and are essentially
lyrical in quality. But it is easy to push analysis too
far; and while certain broad distinctions may be
noted, Rossetti's conception of the subject-matter
of his ballads was so intense, and in expression so
readily rose to passion, that he is always dramatic,
while his sense of melody was so quick that he is
always lyrical as well.

These ballads disclose very fully the quality of
Rossetti's genius when it deals with objective things.
They are charged with imaginative power; one feels
not so much the free and beautiful play of the imagination as in "The Tempest," but the passion and force
of it. The imagination has not dallied with these
themes, has not contrasted, compared, and balanced
them with kindred conceptions; it has pierced to
their very heart, and the thrill of personal anguish
and agitation is in them. There are few poems in
any literature so vivid in presentation, so rapid in
climax, so deeply and mysteriously tragic in motive,
as "Sister Helen." It bears one on shuddering and
breathless until the wax is consumed, the fire gone

out, the " white thing " crossed the threshold, and the story told to its bitter end in the refrain : —.

" Lost, lost, all lost, between hell and heaven."

In " Rose Mary " Rossetti not only illustrates the depth and passion of love, but still more clearly the awful tragedy which lies locked in its heart, to be unfolded wherever the law of its nature is violated. Those who find him essentially sensuous will do well to study the strange and rare setting which is given the Berylstone in this characteristic ballad. But the most impressive and probably the most enduring of all Rossetti's ballads is " The King's Tragedy," — a noble work in which one of the most dramatic episodes in Scottish history is described with wonderful vividness and power. The pictorial distinctness, dramatic movement and interest, the depth of feeling and force of expression which characterize this ballad, place it in the front rank of modern dramatic verse. Rossetti's use of the supernatural element is nowhere more effective ; the lines in which the first warning of the haggard old woman is conveyed to the King on the Fife seacoast ring true to the very spirit of the time and scene : —

" And the woman held his eyes with her eyes :
' O King, thou art come at last ;
But thy wraith has haunted the Scotish sea
To my sight for four years past.

' Four years it is since first I met,
' Twixt the Duchray and the Dhu,
A shape whose feet clung close in a shroud,
And that shape for thine I knew.

'A year again, and on Inchkeith isle
    I saw thee pass in the breeze,
With the cerecloth risen above thy feet,
    And wound about thy knees.

'And yet a year, in the Links of Forth,
    As a wanderer without rest,
Thou cam'st with both thine arms i' the shroud
    That clung high up thy breast.

'And in this hour I find thee here,
    And well mine eyes may note
That the winding-sheet hath passed thy breast
    And risen around thy throat.

'And when I meet thee again, O King,
    That of death hast such sore drouth, —
Except thou turn again on this shore, —
The winding-sheet shall have moved once more,
    And covered thine eyes and mouth.'"

Of Rossetti's lyrical verse one poem has had the good or ill fortune to attain something like popularity, — a popularity due, it is to be feared, to its picturesque and quaint phraseology rather than to its high and beautiful imaginative quality. "The Blessed Damosel," written at nineteen, remains one of the most captivating and original poems of the century, — a lyric full of bold and winning imagery and charged with imaginative fervour and glow ; a vision upon which painter and poet seemed to have wrought with a single hand ; a thing of magical beauty, whose spell is no more to be analyzed than the beauty of the night when the earliest stars crown it. In all his lyrical work Rossetti reveals the peculiar and passionate force of his ideas. "The Burden of Nineveh" and "Dante at Verona" are nobly planned and strongly executed. "The Last Confession" reminds one of Browning in its subtile development of motives, its dramatic vigour, its psychologic insight, and its flashes of imaginative beauty. "The Woodspurge" is perhaps as perfect an expression of a poet's mood as any piece of verse extant; it is a masterpiece of exact observation. Of "The Stream's Secret" Mr. Stedman has said that it has more music in it than any slow lyric he remembers. The depth of Rossetti's poetic feeling, the subtilty of his conception, and the delicacy and precision of his expression are perhaps best illustrated in the poem entitled "The Sea Limits" : —

> "Consider the sea's listless chime :
> Time's self it is, made audible, —
> The murmur of the earth's own shell.
> Secret continuance sublime
> Is the sea's end : our sight may pass
> No furlong further. Since time was,
> This sound hath told the lapse of time.

> "No quiet, which is death's, — it hath
> The mournfulness of ancient life,
> Enduring always at dull strife.
> As the world's heart of rest and wrath,
> Its painful pulse is in the sands.
> Last utterly, the whole sky stands,
> Gray and not known, along its path.

" Listen alone beside the sea,
  Listen alone among the woods ;
  Those voices of twin solitudes
Shall have one sound alike to thee.
  Hark where the murmurs of thronged men
  Surge and sink back and surge again, —
Still the one voice of wave and tree.

" Gather a shell from the strown beach
  And listen at its lips : they sigh
  The same desire and mystery,
The echo of the whole sea's speech.
  And all mankind is thus at heart
  Not anything but what thou art :
And Earth, Sea, Man, are all in each."

The structure of the sonnet is at once the inspiration and the despair of those who would range themselves beside Shakespeare and Milton, Wordsworth and Mrs. Browning, in the choir of English sonneteers. Within its narrow limits and under its rigid laws the greatest poets have poured their souls at full tide into forms whose perfection predicts immortality. This delicate instrument Rossetti has made his own, and after the manner of Shakespeare, committed into its keeping the secrets of his inner life. It is in the lines of the one hundred and fifty-two sonnets included in his published work that we come nearest his personal life. He has given us an admirable description of this form of verse : —

" A sonnet is a moment's monument, —
  Memorial from the Soul's eternity
  To one dead, deathless hour. Look that it be,

Whether for lustral rite or dire portent,
Of its own arduous fulness reverent ;
  Carve it in ivory or in ebony,
  As Day or Night may rule ; and let Time see
Its flowering crest impearled and orient.
A sonnet is a coin : its face reveals
The Soul, — its converse, to what Power 't is due, —
Whether for tribute to the august appeals
  Of Life, or dower in Love's high retinue,
It serve ; or, 'mid the dark wharf's cavernous breath,
In Charon's palm it pay the toll to Death."

With this narrow frame of fourteen decasyllabic lines, divided into the octave and the sextet, Rossetti has condensed some of his most profoundly poetic conceptions ; following the interior law of the sonnet structure, he has carried a single thought on the flood of a single emotion to a swift climax, from which the refluent wave recedes by a movement as normal as that which lifts the tides and sends them back in rhythmic melody to the deep from which they came. Rossetti's friend, Mr. Theodore Watts, has said that " for the carrying of a single wave of emotion in a single flow and return, nothing has ever been invented comparable to the Petrarchan sonnet, with an octave of two rhymes of a prescribed arrangement, and a sextet which is in some sense free." This form served Rossetti as his type, although he uses it not imitatively but with the freedom and facility of a master. The dramatic power, the movement and life which he can introduce within the compass of a sonnet, are well illustrated by these lines on " Mary

Magdalene at the Door of Simon the Pharisee," suggested by a drawing in which Mary has left a festal procession and by a sudden impulse seeks Christ within, her lover following and endeavouring to turn her back : —

> " Why wilt thou cast the roses from thine hair ?
>   Nay, be thou all a rose, — wreath, lips, and cheek.
>   Nay, not this house, — that banquet-house we seek ;
> See how they kiss and enter ; come thou there.
> This delicate day of love we two will share
>   Till at our ear love's whispering night shall speak.
>   What, sweet one, — hold'st thou still the foolish freak ?
> Nay, when I kiss thy feet, they 'll leave the stair.
>
> "Oh, loose me ! See'st thou not my Bridegroom's face
>   That draws me to Him ? For His feet my kiss,
>   My hair, my tears, He craves to-day ; and oh !
> What words can tell what other day and place
> Shall see me clasp those blood-stained feet of His ?
> He needs me, calls me, loves me ; let me go ! "

" The House of Life," described as a sonnet-sequence, is undoubtedly the noblest contribution in this form of verse yet made to our literature. It should be studied with Shakespeare's sonnets and with Mrs. Browning's "Sonnets from the Portuguese," in order that its wealth of thought, its varied beauty of phrase, and its depth of feeling may be comprehended. It tells the same heart story, but in how different a key ! The hundred and more sonnets which compose it are a revelation of the poet's nature ; all its ideals, its passions, its hopes and despairs, its changeful moods, are reflected there; and there, too, a man's heart beats, in one hour with the freedom of a great joy, and in another against the iron bars of fate.

Rossetti is not, like Goethe, Hugo, Browning, and Tennyson, an interpreter of his age; the key to its wide and confused movement is not to be found in any work of his hand. He heard its turmoil only as Michael Angelo may have heard the noise of the city faintly borne to the scaffolding which concealed the " Last Judgment." Intent upon his own work, the uproar of life was only a hushed murmur on the silence in which art always enshrines itself. His was not that spiritual puissance which carries the repose of solitude into the noisy ways of men; recognizing his own limitations, — if limitations they were, — he held himself apart and let the world go its way. That way was far from his, and to close most modern books and open upon " The King's Tragedy " or "The House of Life " is like passing from the brilliant square electric with stir and change, or the sunny meadow asleep like a child with daisies in its hands, into some depth of forest awful with the mystery of wraith and vision, or into some secluded retreat where Love hears no sound but the throb of its own passion, and sees no image save that one face whose compelling beauty is the mask of fate. Rossetti was pre-eminently an artist; one who saw the ultimate things of life, not along the lines of intellectual striving and inquiry nor in the moral disclosures of action, but in those ravishing perfections of form and being which seem to be finalities because the imagination, baffled by their very completeness, cannot pass beyond. He was an artist, not after the manner of Tennyson, whose literary insight matches itself with a melody that presses fast upon music itself; not after the manner of Sophocles, to whose work proportion and harmony and repose gave the impress of a supreme and final achievement; but after the fashion of some of the mystical painters, whose vision included that interior beauty which is the soul of visible things; which cannot be formulated nor analyzed nor dissevered from itself by an intellectual process, but is the pure product of intuition, — something never to be demonstrated, but always to be revealed. "The Beautiful," said Goethe, "is a primeval phenomenon, which indeed never becomes visible itself, but the reflection of which is seen in a thousand various expressions of the creative mind, as various and manifold even as the phenomena of Nature." This quality of perception is so different from the literary faculty as most poets disclose it that it may almost be said to characterize another order of mind. Beauty is one of the finalities of creation, and is, therefore, unresolvable into its elements; something instantly recognized, but vanishing when we try to press its secret from it. Rossetti did not see beautiful aspects of things chiefly, or we could overtake his mental processes; he saw beauty itself. It was not the attributes but the quality which he perceived. He did not discern beauty as one form through which the soul of things expresses itself; he discerned it as the form, the final and perfect expression which is substantially identical with the soul. To most modern poets life presents itself under a vast variety of aspects; the soul wears as many masks as she has activities. But to Rossetti there is no such multiplicity of expression; there is but a single face, and all things are revealed therein. To a man of this temper, philosophy, and statescraft, schools and creeds, knowledge and action, the warp and woof out of which the fabrics of thought and art are commonly woven, are of small account; he may not disparage them, but he finds no use in them; he passes through all this appearance of things, so rich in revelation to others, to something which he sees behind them all, and to which, if they had any power of guidance, they could but lead him in the end. Life is not divided for him into confused activities and disconnected phases; it is simple; reveals itself even in pain; presses back the blackness of the mystery; and conveys the irrefutable evidence of immortality. It is idle to speculate, to press through effect to cause, to interrogate knowledge; the vision of beauty, once discerned, does not forsake the soul, and confirms the hope, alien to no human heart, that happiness and immortality are one and the same : —

" Nay, come up hither. From this wave-washed mound
Unto the furthest flood-brim look with me ;

> Then reach on with thy thought till it be drown'd.
>   Miles and miles distant though the last line be,
>   And though thy soul sail leagues and leagues beyond, —
>   Still, leagues beyond those leagues, there is more sea."

The beauty of the universe, which to Rossetti was both law and revelation of life, was not that fair appearance of things which the Greeks loved with a joy born of a sense of kinship with the thing we love; nor was it that pale, unworldly vision which enthralled some of the early mediæval painters. It was a beauty to which nothing is foreign which life contains; it was in the most sensuous and the most spiritual things; it lay open to all eyes on the meanest flower, and it was hidden in the most obscure symbol. It led up from the throb of passion, from eyes and lips wholly of the earth, through all visible things, to that great white rose in which the vision of Dante rested in Paradise. It pervades all things and yet is not contained by them.

> " Hers are the eyes which, over and beneath,
>   The sky and sea bend on thee; which can draw,
>   By sea or sky or woman, to one law,
>   The allotted bondman of her palm and wreath."

Plato discerned this conception of beauty as an ideal which reveals itself under all forms to its worshipper : "He that gazed so earnestly on what things in that holy place were to be seen, — he, when he discerns on earth some godlike countenance or fashion of body, that counterfeits Beauty well, first of all he trembles, and then comes over him something of the fear which erst he knew; but then, looking on that earthly beauty, he worships it as divine, and if he did not fear the reproach of utter madness, he would sacrifice to his heart's idol as to the image and presence of a God."

To one who is possessed by this passion, life does not cease to be perplexing, to be a mystery of unfathomable depth; but it ceases to press its questions for instant answer, it ceases to paralyze by its uncertainty; the runner is not oblivious of the shadows that surround and pursue him, but he thinks chiefly of the vision which draws him through works and days with irresistible insistence : —

> " Under the arch of life, where love and death,
>   Terror and mystery, guard her shrine, I saw
>   Beauty enthroned; and though her gaze struck awe,
> I drew it in as simply as my breath.

> " This is that Lady Beauty, in whose praise
>   Thy voice and hand shake still, — long known to thee
>   By flying hair and fluttering hem, — the beat,
>   Following her daily, of thy heart and feet,
> How passionately and irresistibly,
> In what fond flight, how many ways and days."

It was this passion which made Rossetti's life one long, eager pursuit, which gives his art, whether in painting or in verse, the sense of something just beyond his grasp, a presence hovering forever before him and receding as he advances. This ideal became most clear to him, not through the myriad aspects of

nature, but in a woman's face; it was not a mere appearance of beauty, it was a soul revealing itself; it
was life removing its masks of shame and indignity
and discovering its divine loveliness.   Like the Bea-
trice of Dante's vision, this face looked through and
interpreted all his experiences.   All the passion of his
soul sets like a mighty tide toward this object of
mystical adoration; all forms of human expression,
the most familiar, the most intimate, the most intense,
the most sensuous, are charged with the flow of his
emotion and cannot contain it.   It ceases to be a
pursuit; it becomes a life.

There is one other word yet to be spoken which
describes this enthralling passion.   One must go back
to Plato and study the " Phædrus " and the " Sympo-
sium," one must steep his mind in the mystical
thought of Dante, to understand all that love meant
to Rossetti.   It meant the consummation and fulfilment of all that life promised and prophesied; it
meant that final state of being in which knowledge and experience and action find their eternal
fruition : —

> " Not I myself know all my love for thee:
>   How should I reach so far, who cannot weigh
>   To-morrow's dower by gage of yesterday?
> Shall birth and death, and all dark names that be
> As doors and windows bared to some loud sea,
>   Lash deaf my ears and blind my face with spray;
>   And shall my sense pierce love, — the last relay
> And ultimate outpost of eternity? "

Before time was, love was, Rossetti tells us in those deep and tender lines entitled "Sudden Light;" after time ends it shall be, or else the Blessed Damosel leans in vain from the golden bar of heaven. Love is "the interpreter and mediator between God and man;" only through loving do we come to full knowledge, only in loving do we taste eternal life. To this great passion of the soul all knowledge is tributary and instrumental; to know is not the consummation, but to love. The great process of life, therefore, involves not only knowledge and action, but the soul; changes one from a spectator or student of its phenomena into a rapt and tireless seeker of the ideal. The senses, the intellect, relations of every sort and kind, reveal the object and develop the intensity of this pursuit. One is possessed by a mighty thirst which nothing can assuage save that supreme surrender of self in which love finds its opportunity and discloses its power. This conception is essentially mystical; its speech is esoteric, but when one translates it into prose, it is true to the deepest facts of life. It formulates no code of morals, but its eternal test is purity and truth; sacrifice and surrender; the passion of the soul which counts all things well lost if only it becomes one with the Infinite Love. This is the passion which expands the vast symphony of life out of a single theme, and presses from every note, however sensuous in tone, a pure and lofty music. Of the large element of truth in this conception there can be no question even by

7

those who crave a different and more distinctively spiritual expression.   To the sensuous alone can " The House of Life " be sensuous ; it is to be interpreted as akin with the " Vita Nuova ; " the same mood runs through both, although one is the word of an artist and the other the vision of a prophet.   Beauty as the finality of expression, love as the finality of being, — these are the truths that give all Rossetti's works and words a noble unity and consistency of aim and achievement.

Robert Browning

ROBERT BROWNING.

THE best minds still hold the old conception of poetry as a revelation, as containing something more and something greater than the individual poet intended or even comprehended when the creative impulse and energy possessed him. The story he told, the song he sang, convey more than the definite truth, the striking incident, the inspiring vision; they disclose the deeper mind of the singer in his conscious and unconscious relations to his time and to universal life. It is quite conceivable that in one sense the critics have found more in "Faust" than Goethe consciously embodied in that marvellous drama of human experience. Clearly as the great German had thought his way through all knowledge, and thoroughly as he had rationalized his life, there were forces in his nature whose momentum and tendency he never understood; there were depths in his habitual meditation which he never sounded. His relation to his own time and the character and movement of that time were matters of frequent and searching thought to him; and yet in the age and in his part in it there was much that was invisible or obscure to him. There is in " Faust " a revelation of the time through its most sensitive personality, of which, in the nature of things, the poet was for the most part unconscious. This fact does not diminish the greatness of such an achievement as the writing of a classic drama; it simply recalls the supplementary fact that as every work of art discloses relations to universal principles and to an historical development, so every artist discovers certain far-reaching and highly significant spiritual and intellectual affinities, which are so completely a part of himself that he never separates them in consciousness.

The poet, by a law of his nature, is compelled to open his heart to us; when he plans to conceal himself most securely, he is making the thing he would hide most clear to us. Shakespeare is the most impersonal of poets, and yet no poet has made us understand more clearly the conditions under which, in his view, this human life of ours is lived; while of Byron, who

> "bore
> With haughty scorn which mock'd the smart,
> Through Europe to the Ætolian shore
> The pageant of his bleeding heart,"

and of many another of his temperament, we possess the fullest and most trustworthy knowledge. But the poet tells our secret as frankly as he tells his own. We are irresistibly drawn to him, not only because he gives us his view of things, the substance of his personal life, but because he makes ourselves clear and comprehensible to us. It is our thought in his words which has such power to bring back the vision which has faded off the horizon of life and left it bare and empty; to restore the vigour of faith and the clearness of insight which have failed us because we have not trusted them. It is this restoration of our truest selves to us which gives the great poets such power over us, and makes their great works at once so remote and so familiar. In its most characteristic singers, each age finds itself searched to the very bottom of its consciousness. The scientists tell us something of our time, the philosophers, the critics, and the writers of discursive mind more; but the poet alone knows the secret of its joys or its sorrows, its activity or its repose, its progress or its retrogression. All these things enter vitally into his life; and in giving expression to his own thought, he gives them form and substance. We learn more of the heart of mediævalism from Dante than from all the historians; more of the England of Elizabeth from Shakespeare than from all the chroniclers; and the future will find the essential character of the America of the last half-century more clearly revealed in Emerson and Lowell and Whitman than in all the industrious recorders who were their less penetrating contemporaries.

Robert Browning offers us a double revelation: he discloses the range and the affinities of his own nature and the large and significant thought of his time concerning those matters which form the very

substance of its life. Burns drove his ploughshare
through his own native soil, singing as he went, and
the daisy blossomed in the furrow, and the lark sang
overhead ; but Browning takes the whole world as
his field, and harvests every sort of product which
goes to the sustenance of men. A poet of such
wide range and such wellnigh universal insight demands much of his readers, and must wait patiently
for their acceptance of his claims. He offers that
which necessitates a peculiar training before it can be
received. The Greeks held it dangerous to accept
gifts from the gods ; even at the altar, men must
give as well as receive if their relations with the
Invisible and the Eternal are to be moral and self-
respecting. They only truly worship in whom something responds to the Divine, and comprehends it.
In the same way the great thinkers and artists compel
a certain preparation in those to whom they would
communicate that which is incommunicable save to
kindred insight and sympathy. The flower by the
wayside discovers its superficial loveliness to every
eye ; but they are few to whom it discloses its identity
with the universal beauty which makes it akin with
the flight of birds and the splendour of stars. It is
only by degrees that the most sympathetic minds
enter into the fundamental conceptions of life and
the universe which another has reached as the result
of long and eager thinking and living. The more
fundamental and vital those conceptions are, the
more tardy will be their complete recognition by

others. A swift, alert, acute mind like Voltaire's
makes all its processes clear, and the result of its
activity, varied as it may be, is soon measured and
ascertained; but a profound, vital intellect like
Herder's, entering into the living processes of Nature
and of history, finds little sympathy and less comprehension until, by the slow and painful education of a
general movement of mind, the range and value of its
contribution to human thought are understood. We
have already exhausted Voltaire; but the most intelligent and open-minded student of modern life and
thought still finds in Herder hints of movements
which are yet to touch our intellectual lives with fresh
impulse, — thoughts which are unlighted torches waiting for the hand strong enough to ignite and bear
them forward.

If Browning's genius has remained long unrecog-
nized and unhonoured among his contemporaries, the
frequent harshness and obscurity of his expression
must not bear the whole responsibility. His thought
holds so much that is novel, so much that is as yet
unadjusted to knowledge, art, and actual living, that
its complete apprehension even by the most open-
minded must be slow and long delayed. No English
poet ever demanded more of his readers, and none
has ever had more to give them. Since Shakespeare
no maker of English verse has seen life on so many
sides, entered into it with such intensity of sympathy
and imagination, and pierced it to so many centres
of its energy and motivity. No other has so com-

pletely mastered the larger movement of modern thought on the constructive side, or so deeply felt and so adequately interpreted the modern spirit. It is significant of his insight into the profounder relations of things that Browning has also entered with such characteristic thoroughness of intellectual and spiritual kinship into Greek and Italian thought ; has rendered the serene and noble beauty of the one into forms as obviously true and sincere as " Cleon," and the subtile and passionate genius of the other into forms as characteristic as " The Ring and the Book."

A mind capable of dealing at first hand with themes so diverse evidently possesses the key to that universal movement of life in which all race activities and histories are included, not by violent and arbitrary adjustment of differences, but by insight into those deep and vital relations which give history its continuity of revelation and its unity of truth.   It is a long road which stretches from the Œdipus of Sophocles to " Pippa Passes ; " but if Browning's conception of life is true, it is a highway worn by the feet of marching generations, and not a series of alien and antagonistic territories, each unrelated to the other. The continuity of civilization and of the life of the human spirit, widening by an inevitable and healthful process of growth and expansion, evidently enters into all his thought, and gives it a certain repose even in the intensity of passionate utterance.   Whatever decay of former ideals and traditions his contemporaries may discover and lament, Browning holds to the general soundness and wholesomeness of progress, and finds each successive stage of growth not antagonistic but supplementary to those which have preceded it. His view of life involves the presence of those very facts and tendencies which a less daring and less penetrating spiritual insight finds full of disillusion and bitterness. Though all the world turn pessimist, this singer will still drink of the fountain of joy, and trace the courses of the streams that flow from it by green masses of foliage and the golden glory of fruit. To carry in one's soul the memory of what Greece was and wrought in her imperishable arts, the memory of the mighty stir which broke the sod of mediævalism and reclaimed the world for the springtide of the Renaissance, and yet to live serenely in perpetual presence of the Ideal in our confused and turbulent modern life, involves a more fundamental insight than most of our poets possess. For the majority safety is to be found only in tillage of the acres that lie warm and familiar under a native sky; to travel among strange races and hear strange tongues, confuses, perplexes, and paralyzes; the world is too vast for them. Life has expanded so immeasurably on all sides that only the strongest spirits can safely give themselves up to it. Of these sovereign natures it is Browning's chief distinction that he is one; that he asserts and sustains the mastery of the soul over all knowledge; that instead of being overwhelmed by the vastness of modern life, he rejoices in it as the swimmer rejoices when he feels the fathomless sea buoyant to his stroke, and floats secure, the abysses beneath and the infinity of space overhead. No better service certainly can the greatest mind render humanity to-day than just this calm reassurance of its sovereignty in a universe whose growing immensity makes the apparent insignificance of man so painfully evident ; no prophet could bring to us a message so charged with consolation as this. To see clearly and love intensely whatever was just and noble and ideal in the past ; to understand the inevitable changes that have come over the thoughts and lives of men ; to discern a unity of movement through them all ; to find a deepening of soul in art and life ; to bear knowledge and know that it is subordinate to character ; to look the darkest facts in the face, and discern purpose and love in them ; to hold the note of triumph and hope amid the discordant cries of terror and perplexity and despair, — this is what Browning has done ; and for this service, no matter what we think of his art, those who are wise enough to know what such a service involves will not withhold the sincerest recognition.

Poetry is always a personal interpretation of life, — an interpretation, that is, which reveals truth through a personality. For purposes of literature there is no such thing as impersonal or abstract truth ; that which through the medium of language makes the expression or embodiment of truth literature, is always the presence of the personal element. The same truths in the hands of Spencer and of Tennyson will take on

widely different forms : the scientist will give his statement clearness, precision, definite relation to kindred
facts ; the poet will suffuse his verse with imagination,
suggest the universal relationship of his truth, and
stamp his expression with the indefinable something
which we call literature. If we define this intangible
something as style, we have really added nothing to
our knowledge ; for in the last analysis, style, as Buffon
long ago said, is the man. Turn the thought of the
greatest poets — Sophocles, Dante, or Shakespeare —
into your own prose, and you will have a valuable
residuum of truth ; but the quality which made that
truth literature has somehow escaped. You have
kept the thought ; but Sophocles, Dante, and Shakespeare have slipped through your fingers.

The correspondence between Goethe and Carlyle
shows the German poet meditating on a world-litera-
ture. Such a literature would be produced, not by
the impersonal expression of universal ideas and aspirations, but by the clear and noble utterance of
powerful personalities of the very substance of whose
life these things should be part. The individual
genius of the artist must always make universal beauty
evident to us ; and in literature personal insight and
power must always interpret truth to us. Those
writers who are predicting the decline of literature in
the growing influence of science overlook one of the
most profound and permanent processes in Nature.
Their conception of the relation of the soul to its
environment is radically defective in that it fails to

take into account that deepest and richest of all the methods by which truth flows into and enriches the common life of humanity as the sun pours its vitality into and enlarges the life of the earth, — that method by which, in the simple experience of living, truth is continually revealed and made clear to individual men and women. Life is fed by unseen streams quite as fully and constantly as by those streams whose courses science traces with admirable precision and accuracy. There are certain truths which never came by observation, which have found their way into the universal consciousness through the secret experiences of countless personalities. Life itself, in all its multiplied forms, — love, suffering, desire, aspiration, satiety, anguish, death, — is the greatest teacher of men. These experiences have more for us than we shall ever find in the textbooks; they penetrate us with their obscure and terrible lessons, — obscure until we slowly grow into harmony with them, terrible until we discover that this education alone makes us masters of ourselves. The potter does not hold the vessel on the wheel hour after hour, under an irresistible pressure, without disclosing, in curve and line, something of his design; and humanity has not been held under the terrible pressure of the conditions of its life without reproducing, by a process of which it was unconscious, the general lines of the purpose which is being wrought out through it. Profounder truth has come, unaware and invisibly, into human thought, through the pressure of circumstances and the struggle of mere living upon solitary and isolated individual lives than through the activity of the observing and rationalizing faculties. God pours himself into individual souls as Nature pours herself into individual plants and trees.

This truth once clearly comprehended, the place and value of personality in life and art are plain enough. Life is the one great fact which art is always endeavouring to express and illustrate and interpret; and art is the supreme and final form in which life is always striving to utter itself. Greek art was, within its limitations, nobly complete, because Greek life attained a full and adequate development; and Greek life being what it was, the beauty and harmony of Greek art were inevitable. The truths and forces which determine the quality of life are always wrought out, or find channels for themselves, through individuals; and the individual temperament, adaptation, genius, always adds to the expression of truth that quality which transforms it into art. Now, of this subtile relation of personality to life and art Browning has, of all modern poets, the clearest and most fruitful understanding. It is involved in his fundamental conception of life and art; and in its illustration his genius has lavished its resources. The general order of things, no less than the isolated individual experience, become comprehensible to him when it is seen that through personality the universe reveals itself, and in the high and final development of personality the universe accomplishes the immortal work for which the shining march of its suns and the ebb and flow of its vital tides were ordained.

To say this is to say that Browning is a philosopher as well as a poet, and that his verse, instead of lending itself to the lyric utterance of isolated emotion, becomes the medium through which the universal harmony of things is translated into song. It would not be difficult to indicate the sources from which Browning has received intellectual impulses of the highest importance; but his thought of life as it lies revealed in his work, although allied to more than one system, is essentially his own. Of all English poets he is the most difficult to classify, and his originality as a thinker is no less striking. It is true of him, as of most great thinkers, that his real contribution to our common fund of thought lies not so much in the disclosure of entirely new truths as in fresh and fruitful application of truths already known; in a survey of life complete, adequate, and altogether novel in the clearness and harmony with which a few fundamental conceptions are shown to be sovereign throughout the whole sphere of being. It is not too much to say of Browning that of all English poets he has rationalized life most thoroughly. In the range of his interests and the scope of his thought he is a man of Shakespearian mould. If his art matched Shakespeare's, we should have in him the realization of Emerson's dream of the poet-priest, " a reconciler, who shall not trifle with Shakespeare the player, nor shall grope in graves with Swedenborg the mourner; but who shall see, speak, and act with equal inspiration."

The philosopher in Browning sometimes usurps the functions of the artist; and the thought misses that flash and play of the shaping imagination which would have given it the elusive poetic quality. But for the most part it is the artist who deals with the crude materials of life and gives them, not plastic, but dramatic unity and beauty. Other poets give us glimpses of the highest truth; Browning gives something near a complete vision of it. Shelley summons the elemental forces out of the formless depths, and they pass before us — ocean, sky, wind, and cloud — as they passed by Prometheus ages ago; Keats recalls the vanished loveliness "of marble men and maidens overwrought, with forest branches and the trodden weed;" Wordsworth matches the evening star, moving solitary along the edges of the hills, with a phrase as pure and high. But in Browning's wide outlook all these partial visions are included. He too can brood, with Paracelsus, over the invisible and fathomless sea of force, on whose bosom our little world floats like the shining crest of a wave; he too, with Cleon, can summon back that perfection of form whose secret perished with the hands that could illustrate but never reveal it; he too, with David, borne, he knows not how, from the vision of the far-off Christ, can feel Nature throbbing with the beat of his own heart, and the very stars tingling in the sudden and limitless expansion of his own consciousness. If in all these varied insights and experiences he fails to secure the perfection of form with which each great poet matches his peculiar and characteristic message, there is certainly compensation in the immensity of outlook which includes these isolated scenes as a great landscape holds within its limits fertile field and sterile barrenness, glimpse of sea and depth of forest, familiar village street and remote mountain fastness, losing something of definiteness and beauty of detail from each, but gaining the sublimity and completeness of half a continent.

Browning's life and work were never at odds, nor was there ever any serious change in his methods and principles. Born in 1812, he published his first poem, "Pauline," in 1832, at the age of twenty. From that time until the year of his death there came an almost unbroken series of works from his hand; they appeared at irregular intervals, but they evidently represent a continuous and harmonious unfolding of his life. He did not begin by trying his hand at various instruments, searching for that which should match his native gifts; nor did he grope among different themes for one that should vitalize his imagination. On the contrary, the dramatic quality of his genius discovers itself in "Pauline," from which, by a natural development, both the drama and the monologue of later years were evolved; while in the matter of themes it is clear that he never waited for the fitting and inspiring motive, but vitalized, by the virile force of his own nature, such subjects as came to hand. Following the course of his development from "Pauline" through the dramas, the lyrics, the monologues, "The Ring and the Book," to "Asolando," no student of Browning can mistake the great lines of his thought, nor fail to see that thought expanded out of thought until there lies in these varied and voluminous works an orderly and rational world of idea, emotion, and action. Nor will one have gone far without discovering that he is in a new world, and that the man who journeys beside him is in some sense a discoverer and explorer. Such an one may sometimes blaze his path in the enthusiasm and haste of the search, and leave for others the building of the highway which shall be easy to the feet of the multitude. Coming to manhood at a time when splendid dreams were in the minds of poets, and glowing prophecies on their lips, Browning held resolutely to the actual as he saw it about him; that noble work of his early maturity, "Paracelsus," marks, with unerring precision, the limits of human achievement. Living on into a period in which for the moment the aggressive energy of the scientific spirit has almost discredited the authority of the imagination, Browning held with equal resolution to the real as the completion and explanation of the actual; to the spiritual as the key to the material.

This repose of mind in an age when many minds float with the shifting tides of current opinion, this undisturbed balance maintained between the two

contrasted facts of life, show how clearly Browning
thought his way out of the confusion of appearances
and illusions into the realm of reality, and how truly
he is a master of life and its arts. One will look
through his verse in vain for any criticism of the
order of the universe, for any arraignment of the
wisdom which established the boundaries and defined
the methods of human life; one will find no lament
that certain ages and races have gone, and their gifts
perished with them, that change has transformed
the world, and that out of this familiar present we
are swept onward into the dim and chill unknown.
Nor, on the other hand, does one discover here the
renunciation of the ascetic, the unhealthy detachment
from life of the fanatic, the repose of the mystic from
whose feet, waiting at the gate of Paradise, the world
has rolled away. Browning was a man of the world
in the noble sense, — that sense in which the saints of
the future are to be heart and soul one with their
fellows. He sees clearly that this present is not to
be put by for any future; that there is no future save
in this present. Other poets have chosen their paths
through the vast growths of life, and, by virtue of
some principle of selection and exclusion, made a
way for themselves. But Browning surrendered
nothing; he would take life as a whole, or he would
reject it. He refused to be consoled by ignoring
certain classes of facts, or to be satisfied with fragments pieced together after some design of his own.
He must have a vision of all the facts; and, giving

each its weight and place, he must make his peace
with them, or else chaos and death are the only cer-
tainties. It is only the great souls that thus wrestle
the whole night through, and will not rest until God
has revealed, not indeed his own name, but the
name by which they shall henceforth know that he
has spoken to them, and that the universe is no
longer voiceless and godless.

Professor Dowden, in his admirable contrast of
Tennyson and Browning, has made it clear that
while the Laureate sees life on the orderly and institu-
tional side, Browning sees it on its spontaneous and
inspirational side. The one seeks the explanation of
the mysteries which surround him, and the processes
by which life is unfolded, in the slow, large movement of law; the other goes straight to the centre
whence the energy of life flows. Society is much to
Browning, not because it teaches great truths, but
because it reveals the force and direction of individual impulse. Tennyson continually moves away from
the individual emotion and experience to that wider
movement in which it shall mix and lose itself; the
fragment of a life gaining dignity and completeness
by blending with the whole. Browning, on the other
hand, by virtue of the immense importance he attaches to personality, is continually striving to discover in the individual the potency and direction of
the general movement. Every life is a revelation to
him; every life is a channel through which a new
force pours into the world.

Browning always refused to break life up into fragments, to use one set of faculties to the exclusion
of another set, to accept half truths for the whole
truth. He discovers truth not only by the processes
of intellectual inquiry, but through the joy and pain
of the senses, the mystery of love, loss, suffering,
conquest; by the use, in a word, of his whole personality. Life and the universe are to teach him,
and he is in their presence to learn through the
whole range of his being; to be taught quite as much
unconsciously as consciously; above all things, to
grow into truth. To reveal truth is, in his conception, the supreme function of the visible world, — a
process as natural to it as the growth of trees or the
blossoming of flowers. To learn is the normal activity and function of the human soul. Together, for
ages past, the universe and the spirit of man have
confronted each other in a mighty and far-reaching
struggle of the one to impart and the other to receive;
until, invisibly as the dew falls on the blade of grass,
there descends into human lives truth after truth according to their capacity. Not by searching alone, but
by patient waiting as well; not by intellectual processes alone, but by obscure processes of heart; not
by conquest only, but by growth, — has life cleared itself
to the thought of men. The germs of all truth lie in
the soul; and when the ripe moment comes, the truth
within answers to the fact without as the flower responds
to the sun, giving it form for heat and colour for
light. It follows from Browning's refusal to break up

life into fragments, that he never dissociates knowledge and art from life ; they are always one in his
thought and one in his work. Knowledge is never
attainment or conquest with him ; it is always life expanded to a certain limit of truth. Paracelsus fails
because the volume of his life is not wide and deep
enough to receive into itself the truth to which he
aspires. Truth does not exist for us until it is part
of our life ; until we have made it ours by absorption
and assimilation. This is essentially a modern idea ;
modern as compared with the mediæval conception
of knowledge. For as Herder long ago saw, before
the scientific movement had really begun, all departments of knowledge are vitally related ; so far as they
touch man's life, they are parts of a common revelation of his history and his soul. The study of the
structure of language leads to philology ; and philology opens the path into mythology ; and mythology
ends in a science of comparative religion and the
deepest questions of philosophy. Literature is no
longer an isolated art through which the genius of a
few select souls reveals itself ; it is the deep, often
unconscious overflow and outcry of life rising as the
mists rise out of the universal seas. Art is no longer
an artifice, a conscious evolution of personal gift and
grace ; it is the Ideal that was in the heart of a race
finding here and there a soul sensitive enough to feel
its subtile inspiration, and a hand sure enough to give
it form. Whoever studies the Parthenon studies not
only Athenian genius, but, pre-eminently, Athenian

character in its clearest manifestation; whoever knows English literature knows the English race.

This conception of civilization and its arts as a growth, as an indivisible whole in all its manysidedness, as vitally related to the soul, as, indeed, the soul externalized, is the most fruitful and organic of all the truths which have come into the possession of the modern world.

This truth Browning, more than any other poet, has mastered and applied to life and art. He sees the entire movement of civilization as a continuous and living growth; and from it as a revelation, from Nature and from the individual soul, his large and noble conception of life has grown. That conception involves a living relationship between the individual and its entire environment of material universe, human fellowship, and divine impulse. Everything converges upon personality, and the key of the whole vast movement of things is to be found in character; in character not as a set of habits and methods, but as a final decision, a permanent tendency and direction, a last and irrevocable choice. From Browning's standpoint life is explicable only as it is seen in its entirety, death being an incident in its dateless being. Full of undeveloped power, possibility, growth, men are to adjust themselves to the world in which they find themselves by a clear, definite perception of the highest, remotest spiritual end, and by a consistent and resolute use of all things to bear them forward to that end. Browning does not believe for an instant that human life as he finds it about him is a failure, or that the present order of things is a virtual confession on the part of Deity that the human race, by a wholly unexpected evolution of evil, have compelled a modification of the original order, and a tacit compromise with certain malign powers which, under a normal evolution, would have no place here. On the contrary, he believes that the infinite wisdom which imposed the conditions upon which every man accepts his life justifies itself in the marvelous adaptation of the material means to the spiritual ends ; and that it is only as we accept resolutely and fearlessly the order of which we are part that we see clearly the " far-off, divine event to which the whole creation moves."

To Tennyson the path of highest development is to be found in submission and obedience ; to Browning the same end is to be sought by that sublime enthusiasm which bears the soul beyond the discipline that is shaping it to a unity and fellowship with the divine will which imposes the discipline. We are to suffer and bear, to submit and endure, not passively, with gentle patience and trust, but actively, with co-operative energy of will and joy of insight into the far-off end. Life is so much more than its conditions and accidents that, like the fruitful Nile, it overflows and fertilizes them all. It is this intense vitality which holds Browning in such real and wholesome relations with the whole movement of Nature and life ; which makes it impossible to discard anything which God has made. If further proof of his possession of genius were needed, it would be furnished by this supreme characteristic of his nature; he is so intensely alive. Few men have the strength to live in more than two or three directions. They are alive to philosophy and what they regard as religion, and dead to science, to art, to the great movements of human society; or they are alive to science, to art, and dead to philosophy and religion. Genius is intensity of life, — an overflowing vitality which floods and fertilizes a continent or a hemisphere of being; which makes a nature many-sided and whole, while most men remain partial and fragmentary. This inexhaustible vitality pours like a tide through all Browning's work; so swift and tumultuous is it that it sometimes carries all manner of débris with it, and one must wait long for the settling of the sediment and the clarification of the stream.

This vitality makes it impossible for Browning, great spiritual prophet that he is, to mutilate life; to reject a part of it under a false conception of the unity and indivisibility of the whole. No man has a more subtile perception of the most obscure and complex spiritual experiences than the author of " Paracelsus " and the " Strange Medical Experience of Karshish, the Arab Physician," and yet none has greater keenness and joy of sense. The world as it lies in its first swift impression on his soul is as divine a world as that which he finds when, probed to the bottom, it discovers a sublime harmony and purpose. Chaucer did not find skies bluer, flowers more fragrant, than this nineteenth-century poet; Theocritus himself, lulled by the hum of the summer bee and the fall of the pine-cone, was not more responsive to the first, immediate beauty of Nature than this deep thinker within whose vision there also lies that ethereal and transcendent beauty which never deepened the skies of Sicily for the elder singer. Whosoever would possess his life wholly must live richly, joyously, and victoriously in this present : —

> " I find earth not gray but rosy,
>   Heaven not grim but fair of hue.
> Do I stoop ? I pluck a posy.
> Do I stand and stare ? All 's blue."

The young David, preparing for the mightiest herculean labours, for the sublimest prophetic visions, mixes his life with the splendid play of life about him, and breeds joy and buoyant strength in the commingling :

> "Oh, our manhood's prime vigour ! No spirit feels waste,
> Not a muscle is stopped in its playing nor sinew unbraced.
> Oh, the wild joys of living ! the leaping from rock up to rock,
> The strong rending of boughs from the fir-tree, the cool silver
>   shock
> Of the plunge in a pool's living water, the hunt of the bear,
> And the sultriness showing the lion is couched in his lair.
> And the meal, the rich dates yellowed over with gold-dust
>   divine,
> And the locust-flesh steeped in the pitcher, the full draught
>   of wine,
> And the sleep in the dried river channel where bulrushes tell
> That the water was wont to go warbling so softly and well.

How good is man's life, the mere living ! how fit to employ
All the heart and the soul and the senses forever in joy."

In " Rabbi Ben Ezra," — that complete and noble exposition of the philosophy of life as Browning understands it, — the wholeness and the healthfulness of a rounded and full-pulsed life are distinctly and unmistakably affirmed : —

" Yet gifts should prove their use :
    I own the past profuse
Of power each side, perfection every turn
    Eyes, ears took in their dole,
    Brain treasured up the whole ;
Should not the heart beat once ' How good to live and learn ' ?

" Not once beat ' Praise be Thine !
    I see the whole design,
I, who saw Power, see now Love perfect too :
    Perfect I call Thy plan :
    Thanks that I was a man !
Maker, remake, complete, — I trust what Thou shalt do ! '

    .   .   .   .

" Let us not always say
    ' Spite of this flesh to-day
I strove, made head, gained ground upon the whole ! '
    As the bird wings and sings,
    Let us cry ' All good things
Are ours, nor soul helps flesh more, now, than flesh helps soul ! '

    .   .   .   .

" As it was better, youth
    Should strive, through acts uncouth,
Toward making, than repose on aught found made :
    So, better, age, exempt
    From strife, should know, than tempt
Further.   Thou waitedst age : wait death, nor be afraid."

Taking up the figure of the potter's wheel, the poet adds, —

> " He fixed thee 'mid this dance
> Of plastic circumstance,
> This Present, thou, forsooth, wouldst fain arrest:
> Machinery just meant
> To give thy soul its bent,
> Try thee, and turn thee forth sufficiently impressed.
>
> " What though the earlier grooves
> Which ran the laughing loves
> Around thy base, no longer pause and press ?
> What though, about thy rim,
> Skull-things in order grim
> Grow out, in graver mood obey the sterner stress ?
>
> " Look thou not down but up !
> To uses of a cup,
> The festal board, lamp's flash, and trumpet's peal,
> The new wine's foaming flow,
> The Master's lips aglow !
> Thou, heaven's consummate cup, what needst thou with earth's
> wheel ?
>
> . . . .
>
> " So, take and use thy work:
> Amend what flaws may lurk,
> What strain o' the stuff, what warpings past the aim !
> My times be in Thy hand !
> Perfect the cup as planned !
> Let age approve of youth, and death complete the same."

The fullest spiritual development involves this joyous acceptance of present methods and instrumentalities of growth and action; to ignore, undervalue, or corrupt them is to miss the very thing for which

they were ordained. One cannot force the process
of growth by endeavouring to escape from the conditions of this present life into the region of the
unconditioned ; neither by renunciation nor by searching can the laws which determine the unfolding of
a soul into power and light be modified, or their
movement accelerated.

On the other hand, one must not for an instant
rest in the life that now is, nor in any of its joys, its
arts, its achievements; there must be an habitual
and unfailing perception of the difference between
the use and thing used. He only truly lives to whom
the falling of the leaf and the fading of the flower
are joyous and not grievous, because they speak of
a larger and more continuous fertility; to whom art,
when it has matched its divinest vision with faultless
workmanship, is still only an unfulfilled prophecy of
that beauty which is never wholly present in any
work of human hands and never wholly absent from any
noble human soul. One ceases to grow the instant he
takes a thing for itself, and not for its use, — the instant
he detaches it from the power which sustains and
spiritualizes it. To rest in any joy of the senses or
any achievement of the intellect is to become corrupt and to corrupt the good gifts of life. It is
the acceptance of things for themselves, or for their
uses, which determines character, fixes destiny; at
these points of choice life culminates from time to
time in grand progressions or in fateful retrogressions,
in illuminating flashes which make the horizon shine

with the glory beyond, or in awful and permanent recession of light, in awful and lasting advance of darkness. These are the supreme moments in which the soul sees in swift glance the entirety of its life, and the sublime harmony of the universe breaks upon it in ineffable vision : —

> " Oh, we 're sunk enough here, God knows !
>   But not quite so sunk that moments,
> Sure tho' seldom, are denied us,
>   When the spirit's true endowments
> Stand out plainly from its false ones,
>   And apprise it if pursuing
> Or the right way or the wrong way,
>   To its triumph or undoing.
>
> " There are flashes struck from midnights,
>   There are fire-flames noondays kindle,
> Whereby piled-up honours perish,
>   Whereby swollen ambitions dwindle ;
> While just this or that poor impulse,
>   Which for once had play unstifled,
> Seems the sole work of a lifetime
>   That away the rest have trifled."

Without this clear perception of its larger uses, knowledge itself becomes a snare to the soul ; it conceals instead of revealing the secret of life. Boundless aspiration and desire for nobler life must drain the cup of knowledge, but never rest in study of its curious tracery, its rich and varied design. The cup once drained of the life that was in it must be cast aside, as the eager searcher goes on his way refreshed. Browning has made this conception of the meaning of life nowhere so clear as in that noble group of poems which have art as their theme. Certainly no poet has ever had a deeper thought of the functions and limitations of art; none has ever seen more clearly the beauty of the art which died with the Greeks, not because the soul parted with some endowment when that wonderful race perished, but because life has expanded beyond the capacity of the exquisite chalice in which the Greek poured his genius as a gift to the gods. That art attained its perfection of form, because from the conception of life which pervaded it the spiritual was resolutely rejected. The life that now is came to perfect expression under the Greek chisel and the Greek stylus; but this very perfection was its limitation. In the art which shall reveal life in its large spiritual relations, life in its infinite duration and growth, there must be imperfection, — the imperfection, not of inadequate workmanship, but of a thought not yet pressed to its last conclusion, of a conception still to broaden and deepen. Antique art found its supreme function in the faultless representation of complete and finished ideals, — ideals which secured completion and definiteness of outline by the rejection of the spiritual. Modern art will find its supreme function in the noble expression of that unsatisfied aspiration of the soul which craves and creates beauty, but never for a moment deceives itself with the thought of finality or perfection. This thought of the office and work of art Browning has illustrated again and again with marvellous beauty and power. In "Andrea del Sarto," the painter of the perfect line, the failure of the artist is evidenced by the faultlessness of manner which he has attained : —

> "Yonder's a work now, of that famous youth
> The Urbinate who died five years ago.
> ('T is copied, George Vasari sent it me.)
> Well, I can fancy how he did it all,
> Pouring his soul, with kings and popes to see,
> Reaching, that Heaven might so replenish him,
> Above and through his art — for it gives way;
> That arm is wrongly put — and there again —
> A fault to pardon in the drawing's lines,
> Its body, so to speak : its soul is right,
> He means right — that, a child may understand.
> Still, what an arm! and I could alter it :
> But all the play, the insight and the stretch —
> Out of me, out of me !"

The duke, as he lifts the curtain which conceals the matchless portrait of the "Last Dûchess," whose life-fountain of joy ceased to overflow in smiles when his command suddenly congealed it, is an unerring judge of the technique of art, but to its spirit he is as dead as the ashes he calls his soul. The real artist is never content, however his genius display its splendid strength ; he presses on, unsatisfied, to that perfect Ideal of which all works of human hands are imperfect transcriptions. Abt Vogler touches his organ-keys, and straightway an invisible temple springs, arch upon arch, in the vision of his imagination, and through it, as through the Beautiful Gate of the older shrine, he passes into the presence of One who is the builder and maker of houses not made with hands. To reach that Presence, to make it real and abiding in the thoughts of men, is the true office and service of art.

As Browning interprets art, so does he see Nature. When he chooses to study and describe landscape in detail, as in "The Englishman in Italy," no poet has a more exact and faithful touch, a more sensitive perception of the thousand and one details which each contribute a charm, an effect, to the completed picture. No man understands more perfectly that the mind is made to see an invisible landscape, not by enumeration of details, but by the few fit words that fire the imagination. But for the most part Browning conceives of Nature as a vast symbol of spiritual force, and describes it broadly, not as a thing apart from human life, but as responsive to the soul in its moments of exaltation. The curtain which hangs between God and his creatures is swayed by many an invisible current of impulse and influence, — becomes at times almost transparent to an eye that "hath looked on man's mortality." In those supreme moments when life touches its highest altitudes, as when David leaves the presence of Saul, Nature seems to be on the verge of swift transformation into some spiritual medium and substance, so intensely does the soul project itself into all visible things, so alive and responsive are all visible things to the transcendent mood and revelation of the hour. In the long range of life the material universe is seen to be plastic and takes on the hue and form of thought, answering the soul as the body responds to the mind. Nature is vitalized by a power greater than itself; and through the majesty of its elemental forms, — its seas and mountains and continents, — as well as through its finer and more ethereal aspects, — its flowers, its clouds, its sunrises and sunsets, — God presses upon the spirit of man; and in the hours when that spirit aspires highest and acts noblest, this vast appearance of things material is touched and spiritualized.

Browning's habitual method of dealing with the personal soul is to reveal it by some swift crisis, by some tremendous temptation, by some supreme experience, under the pressure of which its strength or its weakness, its nobility or its baseness, are brought out as by a flash of lightning. Life is never life to him except in those hours when it rises to a complete outpouring of itself. To live is to experience intensely. No poet is so intensely Occidental as Browning; so far removed from the Oriental conception of the world as an illusion, of desire and will as snares and evils, of effacement of personality as the chief aim and end of human existence. Browning holds to personality so resolutely that he constructs life along this central conception: in his view the supreme end of being is to bring out whatever lies undeveloped within; to seek action, to strive after love and opportunity, and find an unspeakable joy even in the anguish which

9

does not extinguish, but elevates and purifies desire. It was inevitable, therefore, that the master-passion of life should find at his hands noble and varied expression. It is safe to say that no English poet has matched the sovereign passion of love with so many and such wholly adequate forms. Indeed, when one has grasped Browning's idea of love as the fulfilment of life, there are few other poets who seem to have touched the theme with anything approaching mastery. That other poet, whose star-like soul moves with his forever in a common orbit, could have left no more beautiful revelation of her own nature than that which shines and glows in Browning's thought of love. In "Youth and Art," in "Colombe's Birthday," in "The Inn Album," in "The Ring and the Book," in those noble self-confessions, "One Word More," and "By the Fireside," in a hundred other poems, it is made clear that life touches its zenith only as it surrenders itself to a passion whose spiritual fervour burns aways all selfishness and makes it one with whatever is eternal and divine. He who fails to make the last venture, to hazard all for the possible possession of heaven, may gain everything else, but has miserably and finally failed ; he has missed the one supreme hour when life would have been revealed to him. So profoundly is the poet possessed by the necessity of surrendering one's self to the highest impulses that occasionally, as in "The Statue and the Bust," this thought dominates and excludes all other considerations, and stamps the ungirt loin and the unlit lamp as the supreme and irrevocable sin against life.

In Browning's conception of the place of personality it was foreordained that his genius should be dramatic ; should deal with situations and characters, and rarely with abstractions. Thought, in his view, has not come to complete consciousness until it has borne the fruit of action. From " Pauline " to the epilogue in " Parleyings " it is always a person who speaks, and rarely the poet ; the latter keeps himself out of sight by the instinct which is a part of his gift. The subtile genius of a poet whose mastery of psychology is universally recognized has marvellous power of penetrating the secret of natures widely dissimilar, and of experiences which have little in common save that they are a part of life. No poet has ever surpassed Browning in this spiritual clairvoyance or mind-reading, which has made it possible for him to give us the very spirit of the Greek decadence in " Cleon ; " the subtile, confused, but marvellously interesting spirit of the Renaissance in " The Bishop orders his Tomb ; " the soul of debased mediævalism in " The Soliloquy of the Spanish Cloister ; " the first dim perception of religious ideas in a possible primitive man in " Caliban upon Setebos." All Browning's poems are dramatic, and all his dramas are dramas of the soul. In " Paracelsus," in " Luria," in " Sordello," in " The Ring and the Book," action is used, not for dramatic effect, but to reveal the soul ; and only those who have carefully studied these works know what astonishing power is embodied in them, what marvellous subtilty of analysis, what masterly grouping and interplay of motives, what overflowing and apparently inexhaustible force and vitality of mind.   In one of his luminous generalizations Goethe says that thought expands, but weakens; while action intensifies, but narrows.   The singular combination of great intellectual range with passionate intensity of utterance which characterizes Browning is explained by the indissoluble union in which he holds thought and action.   The dramatic monologue, which belongs to him as truly as the *terza rima* to Dante, or the nine-line stanza to Spenser, has this great advantage over other forms of expression, that it gives us with the truth the character which that truth has formed; instead of an abstraction we have a piece of reality.

In his essay on Shelley, Browning makes a distinction between the two great classes of poets, — the seers and the makers.   It is conceded on all sides that Browning is a seer; is he also a maker?   The question involves a good deal more than the possession of the skill of the craftsman who employs approved methods and makes his work conform to the best-accepted standards.   Art is as inexhaustible as Nature; and those who know most thoroughly the history of the development of literature will be slowest to condemn a form of expression which does not at a glance reveal all its content of beauty and strength to them.   A thinker of Browning's depth and subtilty will never attract those to whom literature is a recreation simply, — a decorative art which aims to beguile the senses by purely sensuous melody, and to substitute for the hardship of thinking a pleasantly superficial comment on or embellishment of life. Great art will never be easy of comprehension to any save those who have been trained to the point of understanding what it signifies, and whose imaginations are sympathetically awakened and dilated by it. The fact that a writer is difficult, that his meaning does not play like a sunbeam on the surface of his expression, but must be sought in the very structure of his work, does not disprove his possession of the highest artistic power. Sophocles is still the supreme artist among all those who have impressed their genius upon language ; but Sophocles never condescends to make himself agreeable to our easy, careless moods ; he demands our best hours and severest thought. Dante stands, by the suffrages of all civilized peoples, among the three or four foremost poets of the world ; but the " Divine Comedy " was never yet mastered by the wayfaring man. The fact that Browning is often difficult is evidently not conclusive evidence of his failure as an artist. The great body of his work is perfectly comprehensible when one approaches it from the poet's own point of view. It is then seen to be, for the most part, marvellously adapted to the utterance of his thought, the masterful expression of his purpose. The dramatic monologue is not easy reading at first ; but when one has become familiar with it, does any form of art seem so alive with the potency of passion, so compact and yet so flexible and expressive? Does not "My Last Duchess" tell the whole story, reveal the whole interior tragedy, in a few swift words, not one of which misses the exact emphasis, the essential and inevitable weight? It lies within the power of no secondary artist to match his thought with an expression that is instantly and forever a part of that thought, — not its form only, but its soul, irradiating and fashioning the whole by its own impulsion.

In literature there is not only great variety of type, but there is always the possibility of the new type. The genius of each age creates its own expression by the same unconscious but irresistible development which gives its insight new direction or its constructive tendency a new impulse. It is never a question of conformity to accredited standards; it is always a question of adequate and inevitable expression. The form which comes inevitably with a new thought of Nature or life is invariably recognized in the end as instinct with the art spirit. The style of "Sartor Resartus" is fatal to every imitator; but to convey the set of impressions, to place one at the point of view, which are the essential things in the book, it is thoroughly artistic. The man who wrote "Sartor Resartus" and "The Diamond Necklace" was a literary artist of a very high rank, although he possessed nothing in common with the Benvenuto Cellini school of literary craftsmanship.

The distinctive quality of an artist is that which leads him to use the one form of expression which gives his thought the most virile and capacious utterance; which not only conveys to another its definite outlines, but those undisclosed relations which unite it to the totality of his thinking. Now, at his best this is precisely what Browning does; he puts us in complete possession of his conception. He gives us not only the fruit of a great passion in some clear, decisive action, he indicates every stage of the obscure processes which lay behind it. The soil out of which it drew its sustenance, the sky that bent over it, the winds that touched it gently or harshly, shadow of cloud and flash of sun upon it, the atmosphere that enveloped it, the movement of human life about it, — all these things become clear to us as we read such a story as the crime of Guido in "The Ring and the Book," become part of the intricate play, become part also of our imagination, until at last the marvellous drama is complete in a sense in which few works of art are complete. Browning's view of life and art and Nature is not that of the scientific observer or of the philosopher; it is the artist's view. And those who come into sympathy with it are persuaded that it is a view which enlarges and enriches art on every side, and that the man who has attained it is not only an artist, but an artist in the truest and deepest meaning of a great but ill-used word.

Browning not only sees life as a whole and sees it in its large relations; he sees it always through the imagination. The bare, unrelated fact touches and inspires him; he feels the warm life in it; he understands it because there is something in himself which answers to it; it begins to glow in his thought; other facts gather about it. It may be a fragment when it leaves the poet's hands, but it will suggest the whole; fragment or complete and elaborately worked out conception, the truth that lies at its heart somehow penetrates us, rouses our imagination, possesses us then and finally, not only as true, but as beautiful in some new and deep way. "Rabbi Ben Ezra" will hardly attract those who are content with the sweet and obvious commonplaces of the "Psalm of Life;" but it is one of the incomparable works which slowly distil their meaning to deepening thought and widening experience. Is there not in the sense of incompleteness which many of Browning's works convey a hint of that larger art of the future whose depth of beauty shall lie, not in faultless outline, but in inexhaustible suggestiveness; not in the perfection of form which captures us at a glance and then slowly releases us as its charm becomes familiar, but in that amplitude of idea and of aspiration which slowly wins us to itself by a power which penetrates and dilates our imagination more and more? Life is incomplete, — a titanesque fragment as Browning sees it; shall not art also share that incompleteness which runs like a shining line of prophecy across all the works of our hands? "On earth the broken arcs; in the heaven a perfect round."

In what has been said the endeavour has been to lay bare Browning's characteristic quality as a thinker and as an artist, to make clear his distinctive and peculiar message and work. A poet of such vigour, of such intense vitality, will disclose grave faults. It is the work of intelligent criticism, while it takes account of these things, to make it clear that incompleteness is a necessary part of life. The Angelos are always somewhat careless of detail; the Cellinis alone are faultless. Browning sometimes sees life on its spontaneous side so clearly that he fails to attach due weight to conventions and institutions; he has more than once wasted his force on unimportant themes; and he is sometimes needlessly and exasperatingly obscure. "Sordello," for instance, is distinctly defective as a work of art, because the conception was evidently not mastered at the start; and the undeniable confusion and obscurity of the poem are due largely to this offence against the primary law of art. The lover of Browning will not shrink from the application of a rigid selective principle to a body of verse which he is persuaded will remain, after all deductions are made, one of the most powerful, varied, and nobly executed contributions to contemporary poetry, the splendid utterance of a great soul who has searched knowledge, nature, art, and life, and with the awful vision clear before him still sings with Pippa: —

> "God's in his heaven,
> All 's right with the world."

JOHN KEATS: POET AND MAN.

THE apparent misfortune of early death has had no more striking illustration than in the case of Keats, to whom it meant not only arrested development, but a curiously complete and persistent misconception of his character and life. Of no other English poet has the popular idea been so wide of the mark; about no other English poet have so many clouds of misunderstanding gathered and hung to the lasting concealment of the man. Poetry suffers chiefly from those whose idea of its nature and function is so superficial that they set it at odds with life, and turn its vital, mellow sunshine, the very joy and fertility of Nature, into a pale, unfruitful moonlight. Great poetry is as real, as natural, as sane, as necessary to the life of man as air and light. Of this sort was the greater part of the poetry of Keats; of this sort would it have become wholly had time and growth fully ripened his gift.

And yet above all English poets Keats has been the victim of his feeble brethren, who mitigate their own sense of baffled ambition with the remembrance of his woes at the hands of the Philistine reviewers, and of those sentimental hangers-on at the court of poetry who mistake the king's robe for the king's majesty, and whose solemn genuflections are the very mockery of homage. Instead of the real Keats, virile, manly, courageous, well-poised, and full of noble ambitions, the world has fashioned for itself a weakly, sentimental, sensuous maker of over-ripe verse, without large ideas of his art, and sensitive to the very death under the lash of a stupid and vulgar criticism. It was no small offence against the memory of this peculiarly rich and sane nature that these misconceptions were permitted to become traditions. Although Lord Houghton, Mr. Arnold, Professor Colvin, and other students and critics of Keats have done much to rescue his fame from the hands of those who have accomplished what blundering critics were unable to effect, there is still much to be done before the world, which takes its impressions rapidly and at second hand, is set right concerning one of the most promising men of the age.

Obscurity, poverty, and all manner of untoward circumstances have attached themselves to the early years of Keats ; and if widely prevailing notions are to be accepted, no poet ever had so unlucky a start in life. It is true that Keats was born of obscure parentage, and that as a child he did not overhear the talk of drawing-rooms or play in the shadow of university towns ; but he must be a very self-confident critic who would dogmatically pronounce either circumstance a misfortune. Keats was not coddled by fortune, but he was as well born as

Shakespeare, and with much more ease of circumstance and condition than Burns. The year of his birth was an auspicious one for English literature and for the happy development of his genius; for in the good year of 1795, while he was opening his eyes in London, Thomas Carlyle was cradled in Ecclefechan. It was the beginning of a splendid chapter of English literary history; and the prelude of the deep, rich music of the nineteenth century was already in the ear that could hear it. Ten years earlier Cowper had published the "Task;" and a year later, in 1786, from an obscure press at Kilmarnock had come a slender volume of songs full of the fresh and haunting music which Burns sang to his plough on the uplands of Ayrshire. In the year of Keats's birth Wordsworth was twenty-five, and "The Lyrical Ballads" were only three years distant; Coleridge was twenty-three; Southey twenty-one; Landor twenty; Scott twenty-four. A group of powerful and original writers, who were to broaden and deepen the new tendencies in English literature, were standing on the threshold of the new day which came with them. A group of immediate contemporaries, hardly less variously and richly endowed, were starting in the race with Keats, — some to be his helpers and friends, others to pass him with scant recognition or to "damn him with faint praise." Byron was born seven years earlier than Keats, Shelley three years earlier, De Quincey ten years, Leigh Hunt eleven years. Another group, including Tennyson, Browning, Newman, Ruskin, and

Arnold, were to keep up the immediate succession of men of genius which has been unbroken since the birth of Burns. To have fallen upon such a period, when the intellectual and spiritual tides were rising, when English literature was recalling in the breadth and splendour of its movement the great Elizabethan age, was no small good-fortune. Mr. Arnold has said that in the creation of a master-work of literature two powers must concur, — "the power of the man and the power of the moment." Keats came at the opportune moment, — the moment when fresh impulses were felt by all sensitive spirits, when ideas were gaining the force and momentum of great currents through society.

The domestic conditions which surrounded the boy Keats did not foster and stimulate his gift of imagination; but, on the other hand, they formed no great obstacle to the free play of his nature. If there was no direct ministry of circumstances to his harmonious development, there was no long and bitter struggle to preserve the integrity of his genius. His parentage was humble and obscure, for the poet was born in a stable, opposite Finsbury Pavement in London; but of his father Cowden Clarke reports that he was a man "of so remarkably fine a common-sense and native respectability that I perfectly remember the warm terms in which his demeanour used to be canvassed by my parents after he had been to visit his boys;" while of his mother it is said that she was a woman of sense and energy, agreeable and intelligent, and that she inspired her children "with the profoundest affection." Her son George describes her as "a woman of uncommon talents." Even the grandparents are remembered as persons of marked ability and geniality of temper. The grandfather was in independent circumstances, and would have been rich if he had been less unsuspecting and generous ; add to this that there was always money enough to insure comfortable living, — at times enough not only for independence, but for generous and easy habits of life, — that Keats was free from serious money troubles until within a few months of his death, and it must be conceded that in many respects the poet's youth was fortunate as compared with conditions which often surround boys of exceptional nature and gift. It was no doubt distinctly unpleasant, when "Endymion" fell into the hands of Wilson and Lockhart, to be branded as a cockney and remanded to the gallipots ; but there happened to be no one in England at that moment, however fortunately born and bred, who had the inimitable touch, the rich and splendid diction of the cockney of Finsbury Pavement. Keats had brought his genius to its noble flowering ; and the fact that this supreme crisis was safely passed is sufficient evidence that if he missed some happy circumstances of prosperous childhood, he possessed all the essential conditions.

The parents of the poet had very honourable ambitions for their sons, and sent them early to school. When John Keats was nine years old, his father was killed by a fall from a horse; the following year the mother married again. The second marriage was speedily followed by a separation; and the unhappy wife betook herself with her children to the home of her mother in Edmonton. The grandmother had a fortune of about seventy thousand dollars, — no small sum for a family of the social status of the Keatses at the beginning of the century. The following five years passed uneventfully in attendance upon the Rev. John Clarke's school at Enfield, with pleasant holidays at the grandmother's comfortable home. The first impressions of the poet's bearing and character date from this period; and they show us not a sickly, precocious, and retiring youth, but a boy of uncommon spirit and vitality, — passionate, vehement, impressionable, and lovable; pugnacious to a degree, but as quick to make peace as to open hostilities. He was a natural leader in the school, and even his brothers fell under his occasional tyranny. " I loved him from boyhood," wrote his brother George, " even when he wronged me, for the goodness of his heart and the nobleness of his spirit."

Through this virile and manly nature, energetic and assertive to the verge of pugnacity, there ran a deep vein of sentiment; and combined with this vigorous health of mind and body, there was that extreme sensitiveness, that delicate poise of the spirit between sadness and joy, which goes with a high imaginative endowment. It is not difficult to realize the character of the boy, sharing with his fellows the

boundless physical delight of youth, and yet over-
clouded at times with stirrings of a genius which
made him an alien on the playground, a solitary
among the shouting throng. These overcast days
were few, however; for genius, instead of being the
disease sometimes fancied by those who confuse it with
morbid self-consciousness, is the very highest sanity
and health.

As a schoolboy, Keats cared more for fighting
than for books; but in spite of his vehemence and
occasional violence, he was a prime favourite, — his
high-mindedness, tenderness, and real nobility supple-
menting his physical leadership with another and
finer authority. There comes a time, however, in the
life of a boy of such gifts when the obscure stirrings
become more frequent and profound; the imagination no longer hints at its presence, but begins to
sound its mysterious and thrilling note in the soul.
There is no other moment so wonderful as this first
hour of awakening, — this dawn of the beauty and
wonder and mystery of the world on a nature that has
been living only the glad, unthinking life of the senses.
It came to Keats in his fifteenth year, — came with
that sudden hunger and thirst for knowledge which
consume the days with desire as with a fire, and fill
the young heart with passionate longing to drain the
cup of experience at a draught. "In my mind's eye
I now see him at supper," writes Cowden Clarke, "sit-
ting back on the form from the table, holding the folio
volume of Burnet's 'History of his Own Time' be-

tween himself and the table, eating his meal from beyond it." He forsook the playground, became absorbed in reading, carried off all the literary prizes, devoured the school library, translated the entire Æneid into prose. He took to mythology as a bird takes to air; and he knew Tooke's "Pantheon," Lempriere's Dictionary, and kindred books by heart. No bee ever settled for the first time into the heart of a flower with keener consciousness of touching the farthest bounds of delight than did this eager-hearted boy surrender himself to that ancient world of beauty which lives again wherever a poet finds it.

In the midst of this intense preoccupation there came a swift and momentous change of conditions: the mother died, and the grandmother, eager to make the wisest disposition of her property, placed her grandchildren under the custody of two guardians to whom she conveyed, in trust, the greater part of her estate. One of the guardians, a London tea merchant, seems henceforth to have had matters in his own hands. He removed Keats, now fifteen years old, from school, and bound him for five years as an apprentice to a surgeon of the neighbourhood. From the tea-selling point of view the change was no doubt judicious; from the poet's point of view it was hard and blundering. Keats had frequent difficulties with the same guardian; and as his management of the poet's property was neither judicious nor creditable, it is within bounds to say that his management of the poet was neither intelligent nor generous.

Keats's occupations were interrupted; but his interests were not changed, nor was his progress greatly impeded. Reading and translating went steadily on; books were borrowed and devoured; and visits to the Enfield school were frequent. With Cowden Clarke, the first of his friends of the mind, Keats became constantly more intimate. They were at the morning hour, when the whole world turns to gold. It is easy to picture them in an arbour in the school garden, oblivious of Time and London, — those dragons that waste the fair country of the Ideal, — reading poetry together. On one of those blissful days — Time leaning on his scythe and London grown silent — Clarke dipped into Spenser; and on the ears of the young poet there fell for the first time the melody of that older poet who was to clear his vision and make him conscious of his gift. In the afternoon they read the " Epithalamium " together, and in the evening Keats carried the "Faerie Queene" home with him. Never, surely, was friendship happier in its ministry, or a young poet, stranger to himself, more fortunate in finding at the critical moment the one guide in all literature to the secrets and the riches of his art! The delight of that day still glows after eighty years of change and death, — a delight deep as the consciousness of a great nature, and passionate as its hopes and aspirations. Keats had come to his own, and it was not the surgeon's shop; it was the great world of the imagination, in the power of realizing which to eyes less penetrating and to minds less sensitive he was to be without a master so far as time and growth were given him.

The boy of fifteen fastened upon the " Faerie Queene " with a passionate delight; it liberated his imagination; it spread before him all he had been dimly groping after; it gave his intelligence suddenly all the material through which beauty expresses and reveals itself. He sounded the deep, imaginative reach of the poem and felt its profound and mystical beauty; but he saw also the secret of its workmanship; he caught the splendour that lies hidden in words. " He hoisted himself up," says Clarke, " and looked burly and dominant, as he said, ' What an image that is, — *sea-shouldering whales!* ' " The boy had suddenly become a poet; henceforth all happenings were of secondary importance.

The lines entitled " In Imitation of Spenser," which appeared in his earliest published volume of verse, were Keats's first venture into the field which the " Faerie Queene " opened to him, and bear direct testimony to the deep impression made upon him by Spenser; the influence of the elder poet was, however, of the creative, not of the enslaving kind; it was an influence felt chiefly in the liberation of the young and untried spirit. Thus it is that one human life ministers to another, and the vision recorded by one great imagination becomes the kindling torch of another glow on the horizon of life. Keats was a man of too virile and original genius to remain long a debtor even to one of the masters of his craft; a clear consciousness of his power and the practice that lies between that consciousness and the mastery of his art were all that Keats needed. The first he owed to Spenser; the second he immediately set about acquiring for himself. With the secrecy and diffidence of a youth impelled to rhyme and conscious of his lack of skill, Keats began writing sonnets and other verses, concealing these first flowers of his fancy even from Cowden Clarke, who saw them for the first time two years later. The bondage of the apprenticeship was slowly wearing to its close; but more than a year before the expiration of the term of five years, the articles were cancelled, and henceforth, as Mr. Lowell has said, " his indentures ran to Apollo instead of Mr. Hammond."

In 1814, at the age of nineteen, still looking forward to medicine as a vocation and to the making of verse as an avocation, Keats entered the hospitals of St. Thomas's and Guy's as a medical student. Two and a half years passed in apparent devotion to medical study: during the early months of this period the study was serious and real; during the later months the charm of poetry steadily deepened. It became his real pursuit, his passion, and his life; but he carried on his professional study with sufficient zeal to pass with credit the regular examination as a licentiate and to secure a hospital appointment at Guy's. To go further was to assume grave and distasteful responsibilities and to put aside visions that were summoning him with deepening insistence into a field whose freshness and fragrance drew him irresistibly from the operating-room. "The other day," he wrote Cowden Clarke, "during the lecture, there came a sunbeam into the room, and with it a whole troop of creatures floating in the ray; and I was off with them to Oberon and fairy-land." In such a contention· the lecture-room was certain to lose the day; and yet such was the reality and force of Keats's mind that had he chosen to follow the profession of medicine he would undoubtedly have followed it with high success.

Meantime friendships with literary men, or with men of literary sympathies, had been expanding the life of the young poet and bringing him into closer contact with the world. Clarke recalled long afterward the fact that shortly after the liberation from prison of Leigh Hunt in February, 1815, Keats gave him the sonnet entitled "Written on the day that Mr. Leigh Hunt left prison." This was the first decisive evidence Keats gave of having committed himself to verse; and Clarke clearly remembered the conscious look and obvious hesitation of the shy young poet. Not long after, and on a more memorable occasion, the two friends fell upon a copy of Chapman's translation of Homer; and that same night Keats wrote the famous sonnet and struck for the first time that rich and mellow note, resonant of a beauty deeper even than its own magical cadence, heard for the first time in English poetry. The sonnet has a largeness of idea, a breadth of imagination, an amplitude of

serene beauty, which make it the fitting prelude of
Keats's later work. In the sestet with which it closes
he placed himself at a bound beside the masters of
his art : —

> "Then felt I like some watcher of the skies
>   When a new planet swims into his ken;
> Or like stout Cortez when with eagle eyes
>   He stared at the Pacific — and all his men
> Look'd at each other with a wild surmise —
>   Silent, upon a peak in Darien."

The friendship with Leigh Hunt, which began
about this time, brought Keats in contact with a professional man of letters, who had a wide if somewhat
desultory knowledge of literature, and who was a
passionate student and lover of earlier English verse,
bent upon restoring with his own hand the large
movement and easy naturalness of the pre-classical
period. The result of that endeavour was the "Story
of Rimini ; " in which, with only partial success, the
heroic couplet was freed from the artificial compres-
sion to which it had been subjected by Dryden and
Pope and their followers and given the free, full, and
flowing movement which it has in the verse of
Chaucer and of the Elizabethans generally. Hunt,
who had an almost infallible instinct for good work
from other hands, and who seemed to scent the rarest
fragrance in whatever field of poetry he strayed, was
strong in fancy rather than in imagination. Not to
his delicate genius, but to the ampler and profounder
spirit of Wordsworth and Coleridge, English poetry

was to owe the completion of the emancipation begun
by Cowper and Burns. If Hunt failed of the high
task he had imposed upon himself, he was not lacking in gifts of high order; and he had what is
sometimes more valuable to others as a source of inspiration than great gifts, the literary temperament;
he was ardent, sensitive, impressionable, enthusiastic,
capable of great admirations and of great devotions.
He, too, was a lover of Spenser; and if he missed the
profounder insight of Keats, he brought to the younger
poet a quick sympathy, a keen zest for the delights
of literature, and a wide familiarity with whatever was
most alluring in it. In many ways the companionship was helpful and stimulating; the force of Keats's
creative impulse was so much more powerful than
that of Hunt, and issued from depths so much profounder, that he was in no danger of feeling the
influence of the older man too deeply.

Friendship with Hunt brought him into contact
with a number of kindred spirits, — with John Hamilton Reynolds, full of the charm of dawning talent
and brilliant wit; with James Rice, whom Dilke
describes as the best, and in his quaint way, one of
the wittiest and wisest men he had ever known; with
Shelley, whose name was to be so intimately associated with his own in the splendour of a common
promise of youth and the sadness of a common
prematurity of death; with the painter Haydon,
whose vast ambition was to be mocked by the inade-
quacy of his talent to meet the demand he imposed

upon it for work of heroic type and epic magnitude;
with Joseph Severn, a lover of letters and art, whose
social charm Mr. Ruskin has preserved in one of his
characteristic sentences; " lightly sagacious, lovingly
humorous, daintily sentimental, he was in council
with the cardinals to-day, and at picnic on the Cam-
pagna with the brightest English belles to-morrow,
and caught the hearts of all in the golden net of his
goodwill and good understanding, as if life were but
for him the rippling chant of his favourite song, —

> " ' Gente, e qui l'uccellatore.' "

A goodly company of friends surely for the young
poet; and another evidence that fortune did not
avert her face from the years of his self-discovery
and self-culture!

In the congenial companionship of this group of
variously gifted men Keats found sympathy, apprecia-
tion, and, in some cases, enthusiastic encouragement;
and in March, 1817, a slender column of verse came
from the press of the Olliers. As a motto for his
first venture the poet selected the lines from Spenser:

> " What more felicity can fall to creature
> Than to enjoy delight with liberty ? "

Over the gateway of his career Keats thus acknowledged his indebtedness to the past, and disclosed the
prime qualities of his own contribution to English
poetry. Continuing the tradition of Spenser, not as

an imitation, but as an inspiration, he was to illustrate
the liberty of a new force in poetry and the delight
which lies on the world like the bloom and fragrance
of the early summer.   In the volume of 1817 there
is much that is crude, immature, and of unequal
workmanship; there is much also that betrays both
the vision and the faculty of a great poet : such work
as the sonnet on Chapman's Homer and the lines
entitled " Sleep and Poetry " convey unmistakable
intimation of the presence of a great gift.   The book
was necessarily a kind of prelude to the poet's real
work ; he was feeling for the keys of his instrument,
learning its resources, mastering its combinations.
The magical touch is not present save here and there
in detached lines ; there is little of that quiet, easy,
assured putting forth of strength which later was to
furnish the last evidence of the poet's greatness.   He
had felicity of phrase, but he lacked that finality of
beauty which marks a great style ; he had glimpses
of the world he was to explore with so keen a poetic
intelligence, but he lacked that full and ordered
knowledge which was to make him one of the masters
of the things of the imagination.   The volume had
the qualities of such a mind as his ; profusion of idea
and imagery, depth and freshness of feeling, rare
good fortune in words and phrase, the exuberance,
the zest, the infinite delight of a poetic mind coming
to a consciousness of its power and spreading wing
for the first flight.   It had also the defects of such
a mind at such a stage, — lack of critical power, of

balance between thought and feeling, of restraint and proportion.

When the slender book appeared, Haydon, who always borrowed the thunder of Jove under the mistaken impression that the lightning went with it, wrote to Keats: "I have read your 'Sleep and Poetry;' it is a flash of lightning that will rouse men from their occupations, and keep them trembling for the crash of thunder that will follow." Whoever read that beautiful confession of a poet's faith must have recognized the birth of another child of the Muses; but unluckily few took time to read it. There were other voices in the air, — voices of great volume and of penetrating musical quality; and the fresh note of this new voice was heard by few. Byron, Scott, and the facile Moore were a trio such as have rarely sought and won popularity at the same moment. Keats had to wait, and it was probably a piece of good fortune that fame remained at a distance with that mask of indifference which she so constantly wears for those whom she means later to crown. There were a few commendatory notices; there was a small sale; and there, for the moment, the matter ended.

Shortly after the publication, which disappointed his friends apparently more than himself, Keats left London and went to the Isle of Wight, where surely, if anywhere in England, a bruised spirit may find that consolation of beauty which is one of the most penetrating ministries of the divine completeness to our mortal incompleteness. From this visit dates the beginning of that correspondence with his family and friends in which we possess a kind of autobiography as well as a delightful addition to English letters. It was in the early spring; " as for primroses, the Island ought to be called Primrose Island, — that is, if the nation of Cowslips agree thereto, of which there are divers clans just beginning to lift up their heads." The pain and stress of expression — that deep necessity of artistic minds — was upon him: " I find I cannot exist without Poetry, — without eternal Poetry; half the day will not do; the whole of it. I began with a little, but habit has made me a Leviathan. I had become all in a tremble from not having written anything of late, — the sonnet over-leaf did me good. I slept the better last night for it; this morning, however, I am nearly as bad again. Just now I opened Spenser, and the first lines I saw were these : —

> " 'The noble heart that harbours virtuous thought,
> And is with child of glorious great intent,
> Can never rest until it forth have brought
> Th' eternal brood of glory excellent.' "

He was reading and writing eight hours a day, feeling in some way a fellowship with Shakespeare which seemed to carry with it the recognition and approval of the master of English song, and brooding over the loveliness of Nature, which enfolded him with the joy and exhaustlessness of eternal poetry. There were

days of restlessness and irritation which foreshadowed
the physical weakness which was soon to assert itself
and, in a measure, defeat the promise of the glowing
spirit. But these clouds were momentary; there
were raptures such as only the young imagination
knows. Writing to Miss Reynolds, he says: " Believe
me, my dear Jane, it is a great happiness to see that
you are in this finest part of the year winning a little
enjoyment from the hard world. In truth, the great
Elements we know of are no mean comforters: the
open sky sits upon our senses like a sapphire crown;
the Air is our robe of state; the Earth is our throne;
and the Sea a mighty minstrel playing before it, able,
like David's harp, to make such a one as you forget
almost the tempest cares of life."

These words are significant of the education which
Keats was giving himself, — the education which lies
behind every great career, through which the liberation of every original mind is accomplished. It was
no shallow inspiration which burned like fire in the
soul of the poet; it was no obvious and superficial
beauty which mirrored itself in his soul, and which he
was to give back line for line. His springs were in the
secret places, fed by the spirit of God and discovered
by those alone who hold the divining-rod of genius.
With Keats, as with all the masters of the arts, there
was no separation of life and art; they were one in
that fundamental unity which men never break save
at the loss of what is deepest in thought and truest in
art, — that sublime marriage of which all the great

works of art are the offspring. " I feel more and
more every day," he wrote, " as my imagination
strengthens, that I do not live in this world alone, but
in a thousand worlds. No sooner am I alone than
shapes of epic greatness are stationed round me, and
serve my spirit the office which is equivalent to a
king's bodyguard, — then ' Tragedy with sceptred
pall comes sweeping by.' "

Keats was now at work on the story of " Endymion," moving from place to place in search of the
most favourable conditions. A delightful episode in
this wandering life was a visit of six weeks at Oxford,
the mornings devoted to work on the poem and the
afternoons to walking or rowing. The charm of the
city was on him, as it has been on so many men of
imagination ; and Bailey, who was his companion, records the wonderful sweetness and charm of the poet
during these days in the ripe old gardens or upon the
slow-moving Isis. The months that followed were
shadowed by anxiety. His brother Tom was ill, and
his brother George was preparing to emigrate to this
country ; but Keats kept steadily at work, and " Endymion " was published in the spring of 1818. The
quality and place of the poem in the development of
his mind and art were perfectly understood by the
poet. He had very moderate expectations of its success, and he saw much more clearly than his critics
its defects and immaturity ; he saw also its sincerity
and value as the fruit of a ripening art. His perception of its defects and his recognition of its freshness

and deep poetic impulse were both correct; for no poet ever understood himself more thoroughly. With manly integrity and simplicity he put into the preface to the poem a clear expression of his feeling toward his work: " Knowing within myself the manner in which this Poem has been produced," he wrote, " it is not without a feeling of regret that I make it public. What manner I mean will be quite clear to the reader, who must soon perceive great inexperience, immaturity, and every error denoting a feverish attempt, rather than a deed accomplished. . . . The imagination of a boy is healthy, and the mature imagination of a man is healthy; but there is a space of life between in which the soul is in a ferment, the character undecided, the way of life uncertain, the ambition thick-sighted." It was this " space of life between " which produced " Endymion."

The story was one of the most familiar in that mythology concerning which, in the same preface, he expressed the hope that he had not touched it in too late a day and dulled its brightness. The motive of the tale, with its blending of youth, love, and immortality, had appealed to Theocritus and Ovid, to Lyly, to Michael Drayton, to Fletcher, and to many other poets. Its suggestiveness and its illusiveness gave it a peculiar charm for Keats, and at the same time made it a peculiarly dangerous theme. That he failed to assimilate completely the incongruous elements in his hands is evident; his work lives not by reason of its perfect structure, but by reason of its overflowing beauty of poetic thought and diction. Two years later it is possible that he might have touched it with the mastered strength which stamps the fragment of " Hyperion." Or it may be that the beautiful fancy, so alluring and so prone to melt into cloud-mist if you look at it steadily, belongs rather to the ferment and freshness of youth than to the definiteness and ordered strength of maturity. " Endymion " discloses to the reader of to-day the strength and the weakness which Keats saw in it before the garish light of criticism fell upon it. It has the freshness of feeling and perception, the glow of imagination, the profusion and riot of imagery, the occasional over-ripeness, the occasional perfection of expression, the lack of sustained and cumulative power, which one would expect from so immature a mind : as a finished product it has very great blemishes ; as the work of a young poet it overflows with promise. One wonders not so much at the brutality of the critics as at their stupidity.

Concerning the treatment of this Greek myth, as concerning his treatment of Greek themes in general, it may be said that while Keats had the temperament of the Greek in his delight in beauty and his repose in it, his manner was pre-eminently romantic. He is as far removed as possible from the classical emphasis on form and idea; the " Eve of Saint Agnes" may well serve as the very highest type of the romantic manner. Its splendid colouring, its richness of texture, its warmth and fragrance, mark the antipodes of the classical manner. "Endymion" especially discovers the widest divergence from Greek models. Its profusion of imagery, its mingling of often inharmonious elements, and its vagueness are the faults of excessive romanticism.

After the publication of "Endymion" Keats set off on the interesting but unfortunate northern tour. The scenery and associations of Scotland stirred his imagination to its depths; but the exposure of the journey told heavily on a frame unequal to such demands. From Windermere to Ayr, and from the Highlands to the Hebrides, through scenes touched with whatever is great in English literature and Scotch minstrelsy, and with whatever is pathetic and venerable in the history of both countries, the ardent young traveller made his way, eager, enthusiastic, often in a tempest of emotion, — the mountains for the first time crowding about him, and Cary's translation of Dante in his knapsack. But in the midst of this great experience, the first distinct symptoms of pulmonary disease showed themselves; and from this time, with occasional pauses, the poet's health steadily failed.

The welcome that awaited him in London was of the most ungracious sort. The fourth article in the series on the "Cockney School of Poetry" appeared in the August issue of "Blackwood's Magazine;" and the criticism in the "Quarterly Review" saw the light in September. Too much importance has been attached to these reviews, which are likely to be remembered hereafter simply as prime illustrations of

the fallibility of criticism. The reviewers did not kill
Keats ; and the tradition that fastened this crime upon
them has done them honour overmuch, while it has
done dishonour to the poet. The sin of the reviewers
was not murder, but brutality, vulgarity, and incredible stupidity. That the reviews were unfavourable
and even severe was a small matter ; the meanness of
the onslaught lay in their indifference to the decencies
of life, their unpardonable allusions to personal history, their coarse contemptuousness.

It was inevitable that a man so sensitive and just as
Keats should feel keenly the coarseness and meanness
of the attack on his work, but he did not bend under
it. That it touched him sharply is true ; that it
touched him fatally is false. His was too sound a
nature, too great a mind, to feel more than the
momentary pang of misunderstanding and misrepre-
sentation. His real interest was in his art, not in the
recognition of his art ; and he saw far more clearly
than his critics the defects and the strength of his first
long poem. His friends were in a ferment of indignation ; Keats was calm and cheerful. The passing
depression which prompted him to declare that he
would write no more poetry speedily gave place to a
clearer insight into his own nature.

"I cannot but feel indebted," he wrote, "to those
gentlemen who have taken my part. As for the rest, I
begin to get a little acquainted with my own strength and
weakness. Praise or blame has but a momentary effect
on the man whose love of beauty in the abstract makes

him a severe critic of his own work. My own domestic criticism has given me pain without comparison beyond what ' Blackwood ' or the ' Quarterly ' could possibly inflict; and also when I feel I am right, no external praise can give me such a glow as my own solitary reperception and ratification of what is fine. J. S. is perfectly right in regard to the slip-shod 'Endymion.' That it is so is no fault of mine. No! though it may sound a little paradoxical. It is as good as I had power to make it — by myself. Had I been nervous about its being a perfect piece, and with that view asked advice, and trembled over every page, it would not have been written; for it is not in my nature to fumble, — I will write independently. I have written independently, without judgment. I may write independently, and with judgment, hereafter. The Genius of Poetry must work out its own salvation in a man. It cannot be matured by law and precept, but by sensation and watchfulness in itself. That which is creative must create itself. In ' Endymion ' I leaped headlong into the sea, and thereby have become better acquainted with the soundings, the quicksands, and the rocks, than if I had stayed upon the shore and piped a silly pipe, and took tea and comfortable advice. I was never afraid of failure; for I would sooner fail than not be among the greatest." •

These are strong, clear-sighted words; they have robust sense, courage, and virility in them; they were never written by a victim of stupid criticism or by a sentimental weakling. They show Keats not only resolutely holding to his ideals, but still possessed of that dauntless pluck which earlier ran to an excess of pugnacity on the playground. The reception of

" Endymion " would not have justified so full a dis-
cussion at this late day had it not been for the popular
tradition which transformed a clumsy blow with a
bludgeon into the death-thrust of a stiletto. It was,
as Keats said in a letter to his brother George, " a
mere matter of the moment." And in the calm assurance of his great gifts he added, "I think I shall
be among the English Poets after my death."

And now the story of the poet's life hurries on to its
pathetic close. His brother Tom died, and Keats went
to live with his friend Charles Brown. He was writing
" Hyperion " and coming under the spell of Miss
Fanny Brawne, — a spell which, in the delicate condition of his health and the ferment of his soul, was to
work him harm. It was a hard passage in a life over
which the clouds were fast gathering. Tom Keats
dead, George gone to America, his work spurned, his
personal history satirized, his health swiftly breaking,
Keats was ill fitted to resist or master the passion which
seized him. The winter was full of intense emotion,
of alternate depression and exaltation ; and yet in
this whirl of emotion the genius of Keats burned with
a pure and splendid flame, — for this was the winter
of " Hyperion," " The Eve of Saint Agnes," the " Ode
on a Grecian Urn," the " Ode to Psyche," the " Ode
to a Nightingale." During the succeeding summer
" Lamia " was written in rhyming heroics. At Win-
chester, with its claustral calm and its venerable ripe-
ness and beauty, the late summer and early autumn
passed. " Otho " was finished, and the fragment of

"Saint Stephen" begun, neither with any degree of success. These were the last working-days, and the last fruit of them was the noble ode "To Autumn." These brief months had brought out, not the full measure, but the ripe power of Keats's genius. The apprenticeship was ended; the artist had come to full stature. Not since Spenser had there been a purer gift of poetry among English-speaking peoples; not since Milton a line of nobler balance of sound, thought, and cadence. There is no magic of colour in written speech that is not mixed in the diction of "The Eve of Saint Agnes," — a vision of beauty, deep, rich, and glowing as one of those dyed windows in which the heart of the Middle Ages still burns. While of the odes, so perfect in form, so ripe with thought, so informed and irradiated by the vision and the insight of the imagination, what remains to be said save that they furnish us with the tests and standards of poetry itself? They mark the complete identification of thought with form, of vision with faculty, of life with art.

But this noble power, that seemed in all those months to create with a divine ease out of a divine fulness, was the final energy of an expiring life. Keats returned to London in October, 1819. On the advice of Brown he tried his hand at a satiric piece with a fairy background; but he failed where Leigh Hunt might have succeeded. The "Cap and Bells" is not without happy phrases, nor is it lacking in music, but Keats's heart was not in it, and where his heart was not, neither was his genius. Meanwhile the con-

sciousness of ebbing strength, the bitterness of great
achievements never to be made, of a consuming
passion never to be satisfied, preyed on him like a
vulture.　The strain of genius is a very real thing, —
the strain of an imagination easily exalted and stimulated, of emotions swiftly fired and of devouring
intensity, of a temperament sensitive to every wind
and shadow.　This strain Keats felt in all its intensity.
There were the usual pauses which mark the course
of pulmonary disease ; but there was no hope from
the beginning.　In July the third and last volume of
poems came from the press, containing the work of
Keats's best period, which extended from the early
spring of 1818 to the late autumn of 1819.　Poetry
of so unmistakable a quality could not and did not
fail of recognition.　Nothing approaching popularity
came to the poet ; but discerning people responded
generously to this new appeal for recognition ; there
was a kindly notice in the " Edinburgh Review ; " and
there was a respectable sale of the book.

Keats meanwhile was going through the supreme
crisis ; and no one can read the passionate outcries
which his letters to Fanny Brawne became in those
days without passing by with uncovered head.　There
are confidences too sacred even for the glance of
friendship, and there are struggles too bitter to preserve in any permanent record.　It was inevitable that
this strong nature, holding fame and love within
reach, should rebel against the last terrible decree of
renunciation ; it was also inevitable that this strong

nature should reconcile itself to life and die with the
courage of a great human soul.   In September Keats
left London for Italy.   On shipboard his genius
blazed up once more from the ashes that were fast
covering it; and on a blank leaf of a copy of Shakespeare he wrote the beautiful sonnet beginning,
"Bright Star, would I were steadfast as thou art!"
and containing the noble figure of

> "The moving waters at their priest-like task
> Of cold ablution round earth's human shores."

In Rome he was cheerful and serene.   There were
short walks; there was even a plan for a poem in
Sabina.   But the end was close at hand.   There was
a sudden relapse and then a partial rally, but no more
hope.   Keats was longing for the great peace, and
sustaining himself by listening to the prose of Jeremy
Taylor and to the sonatas of Haydn.   On the 23d of
February, 1821, he called Severn to lift him up: "I
am dying; I shall die easy.   Don't be frightened; be
firm, and thank God it has come."   Three days after,
he was buried in the quiet cemetery where Severn
himself sixty years later was to lie beside him, and
where Shelley also sleeps under the soft Italian sky, —
so near the ancient tumult of Rome, and yet wrapped
about by the eternal silence.

> "He dwelt with the bright gods of elder time,
> On earth and in their cloudy haunts above.
> He loved them; and, in recompense sublime,
> The gods, alas! gave him their fatal love."

The story of Keats's life is also the story of his
genius and his art, for no English poet has more
entirely illustrated the truth of Goethe's declaration
that " everything that man undertakes to produce,
whether by action, word, or in whatsoever manner,
ought to spring from the union of all his faculties."
Keats's verse has this wholeness, this inevitableness ;
it is no play of fancy, no cleverness of mind, no skill
of hand, no dexterity of culture ; it is the expression
of the man in his contact with nature and life. Its
very immaturity is the evidence of its reality ; it betrays no early precocity of technical cunning, but the
tumultuous strength of a poetic nature coming to a
knowledge of itself. The great style was to come, as
the great style always comes, from the full and harmonious expression of a powerful and capacious personality. Keats was not to be a maker of a verse
only, but a revealer of the thought that is everywhere
one with beauty ; and that thought was to show itself
to him only with the ripening of his nature under the
touch of life. What he did, therefore, pure and perfect as its quality is, was the promise rather than the
performance of his genius. " If I should die," he
wrote on one of the last days, " I have left no immortal work behind me, — nothing to make my friends
proud of my memory ; but I have loved the principle
of beauty in all things." It was the passion of his
soul that was real to him in those final days, not the
expression of it ; and while it is true that his passion
has left its immortal records, it is also true that he had

followed the principle of beauty but a little way when
the shadows overtook him.

The tradition of his lack of moral stamina has perhaps bred the other misconception that he was defective on the side of intellectual strenuousness.   The
beauty of his work has by strange lack of insight been
taken as evidence of its defect in range and depth.
Keats was sensuous, as all great poets must be, if we
are to accept the testimony of the nobly arduous
Milton ; but the richness of his diction carries with it
the impression of immense intellectual resource.   It is
not beauty of form and colour alone which gives the
" Ode on a Grecian Urn " and the ode "To Autumn "
their changeless spell ; it is that interior beauty of
which Keats was thinking when he wrote those profound lines, the very essence of his creed : —

> " Beauty is truth, truth beauty, — that is all
> Ye know on earth, and all ye need to know."

For the highest uses of thought there has been no
greater blunder than the division of the indivisible
nature of deity into attributes, of the immortal soul of
man into perishing senses and faculties, of the seam-
less garment of the universe into parts and patches.
This is the method of logic, which deals with the manifestations and appearances of things ; it is never the
method of the imagination, which, by insight, deals
with the things themselves.   Keats's greatness lay in
his mastery of the unity of life and his identification
of the highest beauty with the highest truth.   God is

an artist as fundamentally and much more obviously than he is a moralist. It is a noble and necessary service which they render who uncover the lines of moral order along which the universe is built; but it is an equally noble and inevitable service which they perform who make us see the beauty which is not the ornament of righteousness, but the breathing soul of it.

Keats had this vision of the soul of things; he was no idle singer of sensuous moods; he was a resolute and clear-sighted pursuer of the Ideal which forever flies at our approach that our reluctant feet may be forever lured onward; a passionate lover of that Ideal which no sooner enshrines itself in one beautiful form than it escapes to become again a thing of the spirit. Keats knew the ardours rather than the pleasures of song, to recall his own phrase about Milton. He was alive to the need of moral sanity and power. In a letter to his brothers, after speaking of the "Excursion," Haydon's pictures, and Hazlitt's depth of taste as the three superior things in the modern world, he quickly adds: "Not thus speaking with any poor vanity that works of genius were the first things in this world. No! for that sort of probity and disinterestedness which such men as Bailey possess does hold and grasp the tiptop of any spiritual honours that can be paid to anything in this world; " and he asks to be credited with a deeper feeling and devotion for uprightness "than for any marks of genius, however splendid." He saw with a keen, clear eye who, himself a young man, could pierce the splendid mist which surrounded Byron in those days, and characterize him as " a fine thing in the sphere of the worldly, theatrical, and pantomimical." Integrity, honour, and courage were as much a part of Keats's nature as sensitiveness and the love of beauty.

" I could not live without the love of my friends," he writes, . . . " but I hate a mawkish popularity. . . . I have not the slightest feeling of humility towards the public or to anything in existence but the Eternal Being, the Principle of Beauty, and the Memory of Great Men." George Keats was irreverent, but not far wrong, when, referring to the poor creature which some critics and literary circles put in the place of this virile and vigorous nature, he said that his brother was " as much like the Holy Ghost as Johnny Keats."

Keats's letters are less mature, less finished, than the letters of Cowper or of Shelley ; but they are more intimate, more autobiographic. They furnish a fairly complete record of the poet's moods and thoughts from the early spring of 1817 to the late autumn of 1820, — the period of his most rapid growth, of his best work, and of his deepest personal history. Leigh Hunt saw him as a young man, somewhat under the middle height, with a face full of energy and sensibility, a pugnacious mouth, a bold chin, and eyes " mellow and glowing, large, dark, and sensitive." At the recital of a noble action or a beautiful thought, the mouth trembled, and the eyes were suffused with tears. A strong, virile, sensitive nature evidently ; and the letters confirm the testimony of the face. They show Keats responsive to the beauty of the world, full of generous feeling, unselfish, high-minded, with clear ideas of his art and a large and growing perception of its range. In " Sleep and Poetry," which found a place in his first published work, the volume of 1817, he wrote out his poetical creed, — a creed which he might have touched later with finer art, but which he never outgrew. After marking his divergence from the standards and methods of the preceding period of English verse, he predicted the stages of his own progress : —

> " First the realm I 'll pass
> Of Flora and old Pan : sleep in the grass,
> Feed upon apples red, and strawberries,
> And choose each pleasure that my fancy sees."

No modern poet has been more at home in that realm of the obvious bloom of the world, — the realm of the Greek lyric and pastoral poets and of many later singers ; nor has any modern poet brought back more vividly the fading glories of that realm. But Keats was to pass through that realm, not to abide in it : —

> " And can I ever bid these joys farewell ?
> Yes, I must pass them for a nobler life,
> Where I may find the agonies, the strife
> Of human hearts."

" Scenery is fine, but human nature is finer," he wrote in prose. " The sward is richer for the tread of

a real nervous English foot ; the eagle's nest is finer
for the mountaineer having looked into it." He had
steeped himself in the rich beauty of first impressions ; but he was to make the steep ascent where
great thoughts are nurtured like the young eagles in
the nests seen only by the mountaineer. There were
possibilities of heroic endeavour in him. He knew
what self-denial, self-control, and solitude of spirit lie
before one who would master any art, but he did not
draw back. " I must think that difficulties nerve the
spirit of man ; they make our prime objects a refuge
as well as a passion." It was a clear insight that
thus early discerned this deep truth in the life of the
artist. To wring from great endeavour not only the
achievement, but the joy of it ; to make the agony of
toil contribute to the finished work a depth and ripe-
ness denied to skill divorced from profound experience, — this is to have mastered the secret of art.
Keats discerned a larger world than that he had yet
walked in, a deeper vision of life than that he had
yet seen ; and he knew that these things were to
come to him through the expansion of his own nature
under the training of life, and the enlargement of
his thought through wider knowledge. In a letter
written to John Taylor in 1818 he says : " I know
nothing ; I have read nothing ; and I mean to follow
Solomon's directions, ' Get learning ; get understanding.' I find earlier days are gone by ; I find
that I have no enjoyment in the world but continual
drinking of knowledge. I find there is no worthy

pursuit but the idea of doing some good in the world. Some do it with their society ; some with their wit ; some with their benevolence ; some with a sort of power of conferring pleasure and good-humour on all they meet, and in a thousand ways, — all dutiful to the command of Great Nature. There is but one way for me. The road lies through application, study, and thought ; I will pursue it."

"The road lies through application, study, and thought." Would it be possible to state more simply the conditions attached to the production of the greatest works of art, — the "Divine Comedy," Shakespeare's tragedies, Goethe's "Faust," for instance ? Surely one need not search further to discover the possibilities of strenuous intellectual and spiritual development which were in the mind and heart of Keats, nor how secondary was the purely sensuous quality in which • some critics have found his sole poetic gift. In that sensuousness lay the promise of a prime which, had it come, might have recalled the noontide of Spenser and Shakespeare.

Keats saw the road, but he was not to take it ; disease and death had written " No thoroughfare " across it ; the great nature was to give us only the prodigal richness of its first blossoming ; the ripening summer and the fruitful autumn were shared in other fields than ours.

But how deep was the loveliness of that early putting forth of the young imagination ! It was no delicate fancy, no light touch of skill, no precocious brightness of spirit, which Keats gave the world : it was pure imagination, — that rarest and most precious because most creative of gifts. The ode " To Autumn " and " The Eve of Saint Agnes " are beautiful to the very heart ; they are not clothed with beauty ; they are beauty itself. There is a vast difference between thought turned into poetry, such as one sometimes comes upon in Goethe and Wordsworth, and thought that was born poetry. Since Spenser Keats is the most poetical of poets, because his thought was poetry, — because he saw with the imagination ; and what he saw flashed into images, figures, metaphors, — the fresh and glowing speech of poetry. In this process his soul was in contact with the soul of things, not with their surface beauty. " When I wrote it," he said of one of his poems, " it was a regular stepping of the imagination toward a truth." And again : " What the imagination seizes as beauty·must be truth, whether it existed before or not. . . . The imagination may be compared to Adam's dream : he awoke and found it truth." There is the secret of Keats's genius and art, — the secret and the promise. He left much, and of the rarest ; he would have done more. It is enough that, except Shakespeare, no English poet has found such colour in our speech, has made it linger in the ear in phrase so rich and full. This magical note, heard only in the greatest poetry, is heard in Keats, — the evidence alike of the rare quality of his genius and its depth and power.

Dante.

SOME MODERN READINGS FROM DANTE.

It is characteristic of a mind of the first order that its relations to life are never at any moment completely discerned, — that with every turn of events a new light shines from it, and for every generation it has a fresh word. For this reason the greatest books are always contemporary; they are in vital contact with the life that is, while they conserve and illustrate the life that was. In a noble sense, they are our masters, and we cannot escape from them. They constantly compel us to study them anew; in every hour when we believe we have mastered them, they reverse the relation, and silently re-establish their supremacy. The world has been reading the book of Job for at least three thousand years; but it has only begun to read that sublime argument with a true discernment of its passionate impulse and its prophetic drift. The measure of greatness in a book is the extent and closeness of its correspondence with life; and we must wait on life to discover that which life alone can evoke by fitting the text to the comment, by adding the fact to the illustration. Of no writer is this truer than of Dante, — so long familiar, so intensely studied, so widely discussed. Insight however keen and true,

scholarship however searching and profound, have left
the " Divine Comedy " as fresh, as suggestive, as inexhaustible as it was when it came, without note or comment, into the hands of Petrarch and Boccaccio.
Life is, after all, the only authoritative and final commentator on Dante ; and life has yet in reserve meanings which a longer experience and a vaster history will
break open to the very heart.   When a great nature,
speaking out of that unconsciousness which, to borrow
Froebel's phrase, is rest in God, gives its interpretation
of life, all history must disapprove or confirm it.   The
judgment of any particular age is at the best provisional, and may be overruled a century or ten centuries later.   It is part of the greatness of such nature
that it compels judgment from each successive generation.   As the stern figure of the man upon whom
the women of Ravenna looked askance, because he
had walked in Hell, passed through the streets of the
cities of his exile, a silent judgment upon corruption
and frivolity went with him.   Such heroic fidelity,
such lofty scorn of compromise, such toil of spirit,
searched out and laid bare the meanness and shallow-
ness of current ideals and conduct.   When such a man
sets foot in any community, a standard of character
becomes distinct and commanding, and compels clear
discrimination between the base and the noble, the
heroic and the cowardly.   It is as impossible to keep
Dante out of sight, in measuring achievement in
Verona and Lucca and Ravenna at the beginning of
the fourteenth century, as to exclude from the field

of vision the Alps when one looks at the plains of
Lombardy.

As with the man, so with the work : they are both
come not to bring peace, but a sword. Deeply significant is this quality inherent in every great work
of literature which compels each successive age to
measure by these enduring standards its own achievements. Every epic recalls Homer; every drama
evokes Shakespeare. The necessity of this constant
reference to the master-works — this perpetual return of
thought to them, this perennial renewal of interest in
them — explains the fact that every new age and every
new movement in literature invariably attempts a new
translation of the masterpieces. We are never done
with Homer. Chapman gave us the Elizabethan conception of the old poet, — turbulent, dramatic, splendid
of colour ; Pope, the conception of the so-called classical age in English letters, — smooth, melodious, artificial ; Cowper, the Homer of the poetic reaction of
the first quarter of the century, — unaffected, simple,
sincere. We have the Homer of every recent century,
and we have also the Homer of the romantic school,
of the classical school, of the dramatic school, of the
ballad school. Every age and every literary movement pours an early libation at this shrine. This
tribute is not paid to Homer the traditional classic,
but to Homer the great artist, who felt and caught
in speech something of the immortal freshness, the
tumultuous rush, of life. There will never be a final
translation of Homer or of Dante into English : it is

only to those who live at their feet that the mountains appear the same from day to day; to those who travel they are always looming up in new relations to each other, — they are always discovering changes of outline and mass, as they are seen from different points of view.

This prophetic quality — which speaks not to its own time, but to posterity — is in the man before it is in the work; it cannot be in the work unless it first be in the man. In all literature there is no man so completely possessed by it as Dante, — none whose life and work are so entirely fused, none whose life and work so clearly disclose the conditions out of which the greatest works of art issue; none, therefore, so unmistakably and sublimely prophetic. For the essence of prophecy is not the discernment of the coming event, — the sudden flash of light on the distant point; it is rather the illustration of those deep and fundamental laws which, once clearly seen, once perfectly obeyed, make the future luminous and comprehensible. The soul that has seen God, and grasped once and forever the law of righteousness that runs its divine illumination through the universe, knows the course of events, and can predict to a certainty the main drift of history. Such a soul will never be confused by the glitter of easy prosperity, or the eager and audacious energy of materialism; it will always search for the moral quality behind the apparent success, and measure progress by the advance or the decay of character. It will discern the approach of

disaster when others see only the shows of prosperity ;
it will recognize the coming of empire when others
see only the decline and decay of power.   There are
prophets the use of whose gift is confined to infrequent
moments, and there are prophets whose grasp of the
principles of life is so powerful, and whose insight into
its significance is so sure and penetrating, that history
unfolds before them like an unrolled map.   To really
see God once is to see him forever ; to get at the
heart of life in any age is to master it for all ages.
Such a man was Dante, — when we get the full significance of his life and his work, perhaps the greatest
man in history ; the greatest because of this prophetic
quality, this laying bare of the laws upon which life
rests, this sublime reading of the page of history before it has become legible by holding it between the
mortal eye and that light whence all illumination
comes.

The uses of such a man as Dante are manifold, and
they have not lacked record.   Some of them have always been evident ; others are beginning to make
themselves clear ; others still wait the unfolding of
the future.   To have seen life under the conditions
of eternity is to become in every age a stern and awful judge, a silent and majestic teacher.   Dante could
afford to spend his life apart from Florence ; he can
afford to wait for the complete and final recognition
of what he was and what he achieved.   Our concern
is not with his fame, but with his lesson for us.   As
a poet or maker, as an artist, he has for our time, with

its distractions and temptations for those who touch in any way the ideal, an invigorating and sanative quality. Art is not inspired by art, but by life; we shall never write great books by reading Dante; the great books must be in us as they were in him. But there are moods which favour the growth of art; there are prosperous influences which make some days fertile above all the year. And while the secret of the great artist is incommunicable, his attitude toward life, his use of materials, his thought of the thing he was sent to do, and his manner of doing it, are unconcealed. The greater the man the simpler are his methods. There is no artifice, no magic, no esoteric skill about the methods of greatness; they have the elemental simplicity and breadth of the processes of Nature. " My secrets have been few," said Savonarola on the rack, " because my purposes have been great."

At a time when the men who make whatever literature we possess are under such pressure from conflicting tendencies, when skill is so constantly confused with the creative power, when the noise of the moment makes the silence of the centuries so difficult to believe or rest in, Dante has resources of service such as no other poet offers. An age of expansion needs to study the man whose spirit knew all the rigours of concentration and all the anguish of intensity; an age of many-sided activity and large tolerance of pleasure stands in special need of the poet who felt the flames of Hell blown upon him, and who heard the bitter rain of tears in Purgatory. Not that our age is less

noble than his, or our spiritual vision less true than
his, but that our peculiar temptations find in him their
special antagonist.

What made Dante the supreme artist that he was is
a question which cannot be answered until we know
more about the individual spirit than we know to-day,
— a good deal more than current ways of looking at
and explaining genius are likely to secure for us. But
leaving the fundamental impulse to the mystery which
hides every point of contact between the individual
life and the sustaining principle of life, there are certain things about Dante which go far to account for
the greatness of his work, — which we may accept,
therefore, as the methods and conditions which foster
the production of the greatest works of art. In these
things we discover the prophetic character of Dante
as a literary artist ; prophetic, because the methods
and conditions were in accordance with the law of
fertility and productiveness, and certain, therefore, in
some form, and with the modifications involved in
changed habits of life, to reappear in connection with
all work of kindred range and power.

At the first glance no career seems so unfavourable
to the production of great art of any kind as Dante's.
He was fortunate in his age ; there were " ten silent
centuries" waiting for him ; there was a new world
of thought and art rising out of the long repose, the
rich soil of the Middle Ages. He was fortunate in the
city of his birth, — that historic city not yet enriched
by the loving genius of the Renaissance, but already

beautiful; turbulent with the fierce life of powerful personalities; the very nursery of great minds and lofty ideals. He was fortunate too in that vision of virginal loveliness which crossed his path in his ninth year, never again to be absent from any world, seen or unseen, in which he found himself. But here, to an eye which sees the soil and not the seed, the prosperous conditions ended. The time of preparation was golden; but the time of performance, the years in which vision and toil are one, those sublime years when a man's soul goes out of him in imperishable word and deed, — over these years what blackness of weariness and sorrow; what brooding of storm and strife! Exiled at thirty-seven, wandering henceforth from city to city, from court to court, pursued always by that shadow of a lost happiness, accompanied always by that spirit of fierce indignation and fiery revolt, beset always by the strange face and the reluctant hand, always sore at heart and solitary in spirit, — surely never was a great artist so hopelessly cast upon adverse conditions! And yet these conditions, which would have broken a soul less hardy, a genius less self-sustaining, became contributing forces to the depth and power of his work.

If he had been like Heine or Alfred de Musset, he would have spent himself in delicate but piercing irony, in exquisite transcriptions of a baffled and broken spirit. But he was the child of his age only in so far as he used its speech and suffered it to strike the chords of his soul; the music was in him, not in the tempest

which evoked it. His mastery of his time lay in the
fact that it developed harmony instead of discord in
him; that for its buffetings he gave it an immortal
song. So far removed was he from the weakness
of despair, from the pitiful malady of pessimism
which falls helpless because an obstacle lies in its
path, — that disease of temperament so often mistaken in these days for genius. When one remembers what depths of pride and sensitiveness were in
Dante, what possibilities of suffering were latent in
the very nature of the man, and what fortune befell
him, the sufferings of the whole school of pessimists
and sentimentalists become things of mockery and
shame. They sing out of their weakness, and he out
of his strength: they bend and fall; he rises and
triumphs. "Can I not everywhere behold the mir-
rors of the sun and stars? speculate on sweetest
truths under any sky, without first giving myself up
inglorious, nay, ignominious, to the populace and
city of Florence?" These words were not lightly
written: they issued out of a nature which felt the
constant anguish of banishment. "Through all the
parts where this language [Italian] is spoken," writes
the same hand in the "Convito," "a wanderer, wellnigh a beggar, I have gone, showing against my will
the wound of fortune. Truly I have been a vessel without sail or rudder, driven to diverse ports, estuaries,
and shores by that hot blast, — the breath of grievous
poverty; and I have shown myself to the eyes of
many who perhaps, through some fame of me, had

imagined me in quite other guise, — in whose view not only was my person debased, but every work of mine, whether done or yet to do, became of less account." These words betray no easy acceptance of hardship: they have, rather, a fiery intensity; there is a soul glowing with indignation behind them, ready on the instant to break into a blaze of speech. Again and again the sense of wrong, the never-ceasing heart-ache, bursts through the self-restraint of that strong nature.

> ". . . How salt a savour hath
> The bread of others, and how hard a path
> To climb and to descend the stranger's stairs!"

Never were the loneliness and hardness of the world to the banished more deeply written than in these lines; never was his home-sickness more vividly suggested than in another familiar passage: "I have pity for those, whosoever they are, that languish in exile, and revisit their country only in dreams." That which gives experience its significance is depth of feeling, the sensitiveness of nature which receives the deepest imprint of events. In this capacity for getting the very last anguish out of any kind of pain, Dante was pre-eminent; his nature was as sensitive as it was passionate; the intensity which was his strength as a poet was his misery as a man. Among all those who have wandered heartsick and longing for death, his is the figure which instantly stands before us whenever the word "exile" is spoken.

His reaction, therefore, from outward misfortune to inward power is the more notable. He escaped out of the mesh which the sense of injustice and the bitterness of poverty always spread for the lofty spirit into one of the great principles of art. So close, so absorbing, so continuous was the immediate contact of his heart with the most piercing and painful facts of life, that his work, enriched as it is with world-wide knowledge, rests as directly and inevitably upon life as the mountains rest on the sustaining mass of the globe. Through two parts of the " Divine Comedy " the pain of existence, that mysterious birth-pang which every human soul carries to the grave, never leaves us. When Goethe, a student at Strasbourg, read for the first time, and in a tumult of soul, the plays of Shakespeare, 'he said that he felt as if he had been looking into the book of Fate, with the hurricane of life tossing its leaves to and fro. In the " Inferno " and the " Purgatorio " that appalling wind beats upon us at every turn ; there are times when we shield ourselves from it, as Dante covered his face from the scorching flames that played about him. Never was such intensity put into any book before ; never, perhaps, will such intensity burn on any later page. The book had made him lean for many a year, because it was made of his own substance. No book ever swept a wider field of thought, or imbedded itself more completely in historical incident and character ; and yet no book ever issued more directly out of the life of its writer. There lies one secret of its power, of its limitless correspondence with life ; there lies the great principle of art into mastery of which Dante was driven by his very misery.   Phillips Brooks somewhere says that the only way to flee away from God is to flee into him : Dante was driven by his anguish into the very heart of art.   Everything else fell from him ; there remained only this last refuge.   If he had been less great in vision and in labour, he would have missed the sublime consolation of making his own sorrows the key to the anguish of the world, — of discerning in his own tumultuous experience the record of all human life.   To a pure man there was no other key to Hell.

Dante makes it clear to us that the great man and the great artist are identical : the artist is the man, not one form of his activity, one side of his nature. A work of talent is a thing of skill, and may be divorced from experience, from character ; but a work of genius is a piece of the man's self.   There may be incalculable toil upon it, flawless workmanship may disclose itself in every detail ; but the motive, the conception, the informing idea, are out of the man's soul.   He does not fashion them ; he is powerless to invent them ; they grow within him ; they are the children of his experience.   It is as impossible to separate the " Divine Comedy " from Dante as to separate the fruit from the tree which bore it.   It is so distinct that it may be plucked and yet remain entire, so different that it becomes nourishment for other and alien life, but it is of the very substance of the tree.   Dante's poem has a significance as wide and

deep as any that has been written ; but its universality
comes of the very concentration of experience out of
which it issued. All the rays of thought were focused
and burned into his very soul before they issued in
art. What we call experience is the personal test of
life, — the personal contact with it ; it involves the
kind of knowledge which a man possesses when he
is able to say, " I saw it, I touched it, I felt it." This
is that first-hand knowledge out of which all the
sciences have grown ; stage by stage, art has expanded out of it ; step by step, the earth has been
discovered and mastered by it ; above all, it has been
the road through which those supreme and final truths
which we call religious have come into the world.
They are not its products ; but through it, as through
an open door, they have come to succour and inspire.
It is a fact of the deepest significance that the Bible,
instead of giving us an orderly, logical system of truth,
gives us largely history so interpreted that it illustrates
and reveals truth. When principles are stated abstractly, it is always to meet some pressing need, some
peculiar condition or stage of development. One
aspect is presented to the Hebrew, another to the
Greek, and still another to the Roman. God speaks
on human occasion ; the prophetic mood is evoked by
historic necessity ; Christ addresses himself to the
immediate group, to the incident or event of the
hour ; he uses invariably the nearest illustration.
It is through these lowly doors that he passes into
the region of universal truth. The Bible is, there-

fore, the supreme book of experience; it shows the divine brooding over the human and shining into it, wherever and whenever the two come in contact; and these points of contact constitute experience. This is the method of all the great teachers; not by abstraction, but by realization, is truth appropriated and made a part of human life.

Capacity for experience is one of the measures of greatness. If this line were run through literature, it would separate all writers of the truest insight from those who charm us by some other and secondary gift. The experiencing man steadily widens and deepens with the unfolding of his life history; every event means for him a fresh glimpse of truth; every full hour of emotion or work, a ripening of the spirit. It is profoundly interesting to follow the steady growth of such a nature as Shakespeare's, not so much by processes of thought as by processes of life. For the most part unconsciously to himself, life distils its meaning into his soul through the silent but ceaseless opening and expansion of his mind and heart. Sensitive to every touch of the outward world, responsive to every appeal through the senses, alive to every suggestion to the spirit, intent not to shun but to share the full movement of life, — such a nature presents an ever-widening contact with the whole of things, and gains an ever-deepening insight into their meaning. A man like Macaulay, on the other hand, whom Bagehot rightly describes as a non-experiencing nature, may have many gifts, but has no true insight. He may portray with striking vividness the thing that has taken place, but he does not see or feel the soul of it; he may add constantly to his store of information, but he does not grow rich in that wisdom to which the secret of life is an open secret.

The great artists often come slowly and painfully to the consciousness of their work and their power; but these things once discovered, the channels that feed them are always deepening and widening. Shakespeare might have made good use of the repose and leisure of Oxford ; but he was independent of special instruction, because he was so apt a pupil in that greater university framed for the training of souls like his. He began with the fresh and buoyant delight of the senses ; he read with such intelligence as no historian has ever possessed the long and stormy story of his race ; he brooded over those questions that are a haunting pain to the finest souls ; he came at last, in his serene maturity, to a rare and beautiful poise of nature, — senses, mind, and soul had, each in turn, received the direct imprint of life, and out of that education came the vision which discerned and the faculty which fashioned the world of the " Tempest." First " Romeo and Juliet," then " Henry V.," then " Hamlet," then the " Tempest ; " so runs the story of a soul nourished upon life, and making every separate stage of its growth in the order of nature bear a richer and deeper harvest of art. Not so wide, so many-sided, but deeper even than Shakespeare's con-

tact with life through experience was Dante's. Shakespeare suffered, as every great mind must, in this
long travail which we call life; but he was not cut and
stung by personal injustice; he had the ease which
material prosperity brought with it. Dante bore the
long bitterness of poverty. The only refuge for a
soul so beset was to search life to its very depths.
If pain is to be one's lot, then feel it most keenly
that one may find the very heart of it, — that was the
attitude of Dante. No man suffers from choice; but
since suffering must come, the great nature will drain
it of whatever moral vigour and spiritual insight it
may impart.

Dante did more than this; he gained its indirect as
well as its direct enrichment; he made it contribute
to the beauty of his work. There are, it is true, arid
passages in the "Divine Comedy;" but when one
remembers what material is wrought into it, how vast
its scope is, and how elaborate its scheme or ground-
work, it is amazing that the current moves so rapidly,
and that the pauses of artistic progression are so few.
The whole poem is inspired with clear, coherent
purpose; it flows together; it unfolds by virtue of
an interior force which plays freely and masterfully
through every part of it, and gives it unity of structure and of beauty no less than unity of idea. To
achieve this supreme effect of art, this fusion of materials, this perfection of form, a supreme effort of
the whole nature is demanded: this kind cometh not
save by prayer and fasting. The steady concentra-

tion of mind involved in such a work is a moral achievement of the highest order; the patient brooding over the theme, tracing its relations through wide fields of knowledge and history, detecting its analogies and illustrations in the sequence of human and natural fact and law, is an intellectual achievement possible only to the greatest minds. Art is mastered not by the violent, but by the self-sacrificing, the patient, and the enduring. It does not respond to half-hearted devotion; it is won by no intermittent service; it tolerates no compromise with pleasure, with conventions, with other and alien aims and occupations. The painter who is half-artist and half-courtier secures his easy popularity, his quick returns, his social successes, his luxury; but amid all the applauding voices that reach him he listens in vain for the incorruptible voice of fame. To Michael Angelo, silent and solitary on his lonely scaffolding, sternly intent upon his task, sternly indifferent to the praise of the palace or the cheer of the square, that voice came clear and sustaining. Many wait for the sound of that voice; but it is heard by those only who shut their souls against all other and lesser voices. Dante heard that voice. Sounds that mingle with most lives, sounds sweet with the long usage of affection, and dear to the heart that leans on familiar things, were denied him; but he had for consolation and companionship this voice borne in from the unborn times and the unborn men. There was a singleness of aim in him, matched with a sustained devotion, which gathered all the forces of his

nature in one continuous and absorbing task. Shut
off from complicated relations with his time, excluded
from the privileges and cares of citizenship, practically without family ties, he poured the undivided
stream of his power and activity into a single channel.
It was not his mind alone which was engaged in his
work ; it was not heart alone ; it was not his technical
skill and the energy of his nature : in the blending
of all these qualities is found the secret of that intensity which gives the " Divine Comedy " unity of
feeling through all its vast movement. Ballads and
lyrics often breathe a single fiery emotion ; but there
is no other poem of equal magnitude which glows
with such sustained heat of soul.

A work of art is great in the exact measure in which
it absorbs and receives the life of the artist, — in the
measure in which it springs, as Goethe would say,
from the union of all his faculties. It may be strong,
original, suggestive, if it come primarily from his mind ;
it may be moving, inspiring, impressive, if it flow
from his heart alone ; it may be clear, effective, beautiful, if it be the product of his skill or training ; but it
is great, deep, and enduring in the measure in which
all these faculties and forces contribute to and are
mingled in it. It is this fusion of his whole nature
which gives Dante's work not only unity, but such
range and variety. He had the equipment of a
thinker of the first order ; and if his mind had been
primarily engaged in his work, he would have added
another to the massive folios and quartos of the school-

man ; there is a whole system of philosophy in the
" Divine Comedy." He had the quick imagination,
the glowing feeling, of the lyrical poet ; if his heart
had been primarily engaged in his work, we should
have had another poet of pure song ; that vision of
the fated lovers floating over the blackness of Hell
remains the matchless revelation of a heart that knew
all the tenderness and bitterness of love. He had
the constructive genius, the ripe culture, the technical
training, which make an artist by instinct and necessity ; if his skill had been the chief quality in his
work, we should have had more art for art's sake.
We have the " Divine Comedy " because none of
these separate faculties took the lead : they flowed together ; the whole man was involved and expressed
in the work.

In the very nature of Dante's undertaking lay an
all but insurmountable task ; it was so large in scheme,
it involved so much knowledge, it demanded such
elaboration, such proportion, such adjustment. The
Homeric poems had the great aid of successive episodes and incidents, even when continuous narrative
failed them ; the Greek tragedies had in each case a
living germ of myth or history ; the " Epic of Kings,"
the " Kalevala," the " Nibelungen Lied," ran close
to legend or tradition. Shakespeare's power shows
no sign of limitation ; but the plays, while they bring
the whole movement of life within the vision of the
imagination, are for a narrow stage and for a brief
three hours. There were pauses of rest between the

writing of them : the theme changed; the mind addressed itself to new problems; there was vast variation of material and of treatment, — as, for instance, between " Lear " and " Antony and Cleopatra." But Dante had no such aids from legend or history, from myth or story, from change and variety of work. No man ever owed more to history than he ; but history did not aid him with narrative ease and flow : his theme shifted the stage of its unfolding ; but it is, after all, the same theme in Hell, in Purgatory, and in Paradise. All things considered, the " Divine Comedy " is the most tremendous task ever undertaken by a poet, — a task demanding not greater genius, perhaps, than some other tasks, but greater fixity of attention, more prolonged and continuous absorption, more stern and resolute severance from affairs. Dante's success was conditioned upon long detachment, upon unbroken absorption, upon the concentration and fusion of his whole nature. His success has, therefore, a moral and intellectual significance practically unique in literature. He illustrates in himself the laws of success as impressively and as authoritatively as his work discloses the standards and aims of art. To possess Dante's genius is not enough; one must possess also Dante's power of sacrifice and fervour of consecration. To write the " Divine Comedy," one must not only live for art, but, in a very true sense, die for it. A large part of the poet's happiness and all his ease and comfort, the things that in a way console the body for the sorrows of the spirit, — were lost in the doing of that sublime work. There were great inspirations, and consolations by the way ; but let no man count the sacrifice less because the work to which it contributed is so noble. To underestimate the suffering of the heart is to lessen the significance of the achievement and rob it of its supreme dignity. The law which wrought such havoc with Dante's personal happiness has constant illustration in every field of endeavour ; but men are slow to learn and quick to forget it. It is part of the open secret which so many fail to read, though it lies written over all tasks and careers. Whosoever would find his life must lose it, whosoever would keep must spend, whosoever would achieve must fail ; subblime paradox of the human life in which the divine is always mingling and striving for the mastery !

Dante may well stand as the typical artist in the completeness of his surrender to his art ; he poured out his life as a libation to the Muse of poetry, — that beautiful mistress of the imagination, radiant with imperishable charms, possessed of such glorious rewards, and yet so inexorable in her demand for devotion ! The men who have risen to the height of this consecration have, through this very surrender, made themselves masters of life and its arts of expression. Æschylus sustained this test, and the older Greece lives in his work ; Shakespeare was equal to this demand, and left us what have well been called the most authentic documents of human history; Goethe, in his way, rose to this exalted plane of sustained endeavour, and the modern world was foreshadowed in his prose and verse. Byron, on the other hand, with his unsurpassed gift of lyric expression, failed of this supreme surrender, and failed also of the complete expression of his genius. Of how many richly endowed poets must the same record be made! They possessed all the materials for work of the highest quality, of the greatest magnitude; they wrought at times with a fidelity that made the occasional moments what the years ought to have been: but lacking the power of sustained endeavour born of the union of spiritual integrity with intellectual force, they missed that putting forth of the whole nature in unbroken continuity which is the inexorable law of supreme achievement. In art, which in its deepest aspects is but another name for religion, a man cannot serve two masters. He who sets himself to the task of interpreting life on any great scale must put the world, the flesh, and the Devil behind him as resolutely as ever anchorite shut the door of his cell in the face of these tempters from the perfect way. It is idle to talk of a disseverance between great art and fundamental morals: they are not bound together by external law; they are as soil and fruit, as sun and light, as truth and beauty. A sound nature, a mind moving inevitably to appointed ends, a whole man, — these are the only sources of the work which sustains comparison with the soundness and inevitableness of Nature. The swallow-flights of song, touching things near and familiar, have their truth and their sweetness; but it is the enduring strength of the eagle's wing that holds a steady way between the light and the world which it searches and reveals. Durante Alighieri, the poet's baptismal name, — the " enduring one," and the " wing-bearer," — reveals the secret of this masterful soul.

Probably no poem was ever more thoroughly thought out, so far as its general plan, the relation of its parts, and the blending of its different but harmonious ends were concerned, than the " Divine Comedy." In large design and in minute detail, it is characterized by marvellous definiteness. Every outline is distinct, every personage unerringly described ; the adjectives seem often welded to the substantives ; nothing is left unfinished. From the beginning to the end of his journey, Dante seems to have known where the next step would take him ; and yet, in spite of this extraordinary grasp and clearness of intention, the " Divine Comedy " owes more to the unconscious than to the conscious Dante, — more to the poet's nature than to his mind. The poem has been spoken of as a task ; and when one studies it from the analytical standpoint, the writing of it is seen to have been one of the greatest tasks ever undertaken. There is another point of view, however, from which this massive work loses the elements of a task, and takes on the aspects of play. There are in it the ease, the freedom, the fulness, of a great nature dealing with life as a master, not as a servant, and creating not arduously, but from an inward pressure. The " Divine Comedy " was not made; it grew. There was a vital process behind it. There were all the stages of growth in its production from the moment when the seed began to germinate in the soil to that hour — the purest, divinest that art has ever known — when it bore the white rose in Paradise. It was not the tremendous effort of a mind strained to the last point of endurance; it was the overflow of a nature through which the tidal influences and forces of life flowed deep and strong. To borrow Ruskin's thought, it is not a great effort, but a great force, which we feel in the " Divine Comedy." A thing of skill, contrivance, mechanism, is detached from its maker and its surroundings; a thing of life is rooted in the soil where it grows. Behind every flower there are the earth and the heavens, and the most secluded violet involves them both; it could not have been without their combined ministry to its fragile life. Behind Westminster Abbey there were not only stone quarries and tools, there were religion, art, history, fathomless depths of faith and service. Behind the " Divine Comedy " there is more than Dante was conscious of, clear as his intention was and definite as was his plan. It was a beautiful fancy of the Greeks that the gods were sometimes surprised in their solitude, — Diana at her bath, and Pan on the road to Sparta; but it was only a fancy. The imagination — that larger and deeper insight — knows that divinity cannot be seen by eyes that depend for their seeing upon a waxing and waning light; it is the inward and constant light that

shines upon God, and we see him and still live. Not
only are we hidden from each other, but we are hidden from ourselves; that is our sacredness. We
are fed by unseen springs through invisible channels.
We are as conscious at times of the advance and recession of tides of power as we are of the incom-
ing and outgoing of the ocean currents. There are
depths in us which we cannot sound; race instincts
which ally us with the remotest past; ancient associations with forest and sea which survive the memory of
their origin; affinities with Nature which keep us in
touch with a world of force and beauty which we
never fully comprehend, but with which we have a
mysterious intimacy. All history seems to echo and
reverberate within us; its oldest stories are strangely
familiar. More wonderful even than this complexity
and vitality of natural and human association and influence are the contacts between our souls and the
Soul of the universe.

Now, the greater a nature, the wider its sweep of
these unrecorded experiences, the deeper its rootage
in this mysterious soil of history, race, nature, divinity.
When such a nature produces in the field of art, that
which grows out of it will gather up and reproduce a
vitality far greater and more significant than the artist
standing alone could contribute to it. It is for this
reason that a few men are recognized as speaking for
their races; a whole section of life, a long movement
of history, seem to bear in them the flower of expression. These men produce out of their unconscious-

ness far more than out of their consciousness ; they see clearly enough the point to which they would go ; but while we journey with them the earth and the heavens are unrolled before us ; the road along which we pass is but a faintly marked line across unexplored continents.   Dante has very definite things to say ; but his deepest message is to the imagination, and is therefore unspoken.   His song is " unfathomable," as Tieck long ago called it, because all life flows under it. Here, again, we come upon his prophetic quality, — his foreshadowing of the attitude and method of the true artist in all times.   That which the artist gives us is himself.   His genius is not his ; it belongs to the world, because the world has contributed the material with which it deals.   No man ever owed more to his fellows than Dante.   Shakespeare borrowed stories from all quarters ; Dante borrowed all history. The " Divine Comedy" is embedded in history ; its background is the entire historic movement.   It was Dante's greatness that his life had such reach and force, — that it gathered into itself so vast a range of experience, and brought to light so wide a sweep of action.   These facts of history had long sunk below the region of consciousness in him ; he had absorbed the past and made it part of himself before he expressed the soul of it in poetry.   The Middle Ages had, for the purposes of art, this priceless quality of unconsciousness.   Morbid as mediæval thought often was, distorted as its imagination was, grotesque as its mistakes of fact often were, it had a *naïveté* and unconsciousness which we sadly and fatally lack. The mediæval spirit thought much, but it thought passionately, with a certain fervour and intensity; it thought largely by the aid of the imagination. It felt more than it thought; and in art feeling is the essential quality. Thought without feeling gives us philosophy or science; thought with feeling gives us literature. The mediæval spirit felt deeply and instinctively, and so, without consciousness of the process, it produced a vast growth of popular epics, songs, and stories; and its reverence and piety, felt to the very depths of its nature, were set in pillar and arch, in window and fretted roof, in the imperishable beauty of the cathedral.

Dante was the first great literary nature touched by these hidden streams of faith and beauty. He not only shared in them, but by so much as he was greater than his contemporaries he was fed by them. He was one of the deepest and clearest of the mediæval thinkers; but he felt more profoundly than he thought. Thought, knowledge, fact, were never cold to him; they seemed to burn their way into his mind; they sank through his mind into his heart. It was one of the superstitions of the time that cities were sometimes sunk by magicians into the depths of pools; and the peasant passing by at dusk peered trembling and awestruck into the still waters, and saw there the lost town swallowed up in death and silence, — the streets empty that had once been thronged; the bells silent that had once swung with resonant melody; the houses

deserted that had once had cheer and mirth of life.
So in Dante that old world survives, and we read it
to the very heart.   It is not until thought, knowledge,
and fact pass beyond the mind into the keeping of
the heart, where feeling plays upon them and divines
their spiritual meanings, that art finds them ripe for
use.   The first perceptions of unsuspected beauty in
things is always accompanied by agitation.   The very
essence of literature is this sensitiveness of perception,
this freshness of feeling, which clothes familiar facts
and obvious truths with a loveliness or majesty un-
dreamed of by the thought alone.   It is through the
insight and play of the imagination that the historic
fact yields its inner and spiritual meaning ; and there
must be a brooding of the whole nature over the fact
before it ripens into art.   While questions are still
pressing for answer, while movements still absorb the
faculties in action, while problems still agitate and dis-
turb, they rarely receive literary expression.   When
the struggle is over and the movement accomplished,
the Muse of Poetry comes to claim her own.   The
agony of strife yields to the quiet meditation, the
mysterious distillation of truth, the deep and sweet disclosure of beauty.   Far below the region of eager and
painful thinking, with its unrest and its agitation, the
question, the problem, the great issues, sink into the
rich, profound, unconscious life of a people or a man.
They become a kind of background, full of majesty,
of mystery, of suggestion and allurement for the
imagination, — like those mountain-ranges which

guarded the youth of Titian, and in the long years of his maturity appeared and reappeared in his works. For this reason childhood is so often and so incomparably touched by the great writers. It lies behind them, a real landscape, but with what softness of outline, what mysteries of light and atmosphere !

Dante came when this light lay soft on the "ten silent centuries," — when their tasks were done and their service complete ; when the problems that had tormented faithful and morbid souls alike were settled ; when the new era was at hand, and the new world was rising out of the old. Deep in the heart and memory of that old world lay the records and experiences of its youth and its prime ; deep in Dante's heart they waited for the discernment of his deep intelligence, for the expression of his unsurpassed faculty of song. He carried that old world in his heart through all his wanderings; he brooded over it until its faith, its art, its history, were fused, harmonized, and completely possessed. When the "Divine Comedy" grew under his hands, this ripe and rich past, this vast and fathomless life, to which races and centuries had contributed, rose into consciousness once more, — rose in organic unity and completeness, with such disclosure of far-reaching spiritual relations, of immortal significance to the soul of man, as only a poet who was also a prophet could give it. It was no longer an abstract faith, an arbitrary knowledge, a mass of unrelated facts; it was the allegory of the soul's pilgrimage, the revelation of the soul's life.

There is but one " Divine Comedy," — one poem in which depth and height of thought, beauty of form, and intensity of feeling are so perfectly combined. There are only three or four works in all literature which we place beside this poem. It has less breadth, less range of sunny fruitfulness, than the work of Shakespeare and of Goethe ; but it is the highest altitude of human achievement. It is one of the great satisfactions of humanity, because it realizes the noblest anticipations of life. Here was a man who lived in the heart of things, who thought and acted as if he were conscious of immortality ; who could afford to let one phase of life torment and disown him, because he had all life for compensation ; who lived and wrought like a master, born to the highest intellectual and spiritual possessions, and not to be despoiled of them by any chance of earthly fortune. All men crave such living and performance as Dante's, because they adequately express the energy of an immortal spirit. Scepticism, cynicism, pessimism, have their periods ; the race has its bad quarter of an hour now and then ; but such men as Dante make these ignoble suspicions of divinity, these mean doubts about our fellows, these weak denials of our own natures, incredible. One righteous man demonstrates the reality of goodness, and one great man makes all life great. Scepticism is the root of all evil in us and in our arts. We do not believe enough in God, in ourselves, and in the divine laws under which we live. Great art involves great faith, — a clear, resolute, victorious insight into and grasp of things; a belief real enough and powerful enough to inspire and sustain heroic tasks. The open secret of a great and noble achievement in art is a sound and noble nature in the artist. Dante was great in himself, — not faultless, not entirely harmonious, but great in faith, in force, and in endeavour. He met life as a strong swimmer meets the sea, not with dismay and outcries, but with heroic putting forth of effort, with calmness and steadiness of soul, with the buoyancy of a great strength matching itself against a great peril. He believed and he achieved, — that is the true story of his life.

A WORD ABOUT HUMOUR.

THE difficulties which beset the endeavour to define vital qualities are very evident in the results of the attempts, dating back to the time of Aristotle, to draw sharp lines of distinction between wit and humour. Literature does not offer the record of a more delightful will-o'-the-wisp pursuit. These pervasive elements are present in every literature ; but they have a Protean variability of form, and they sport with severe and logical thinkers with an easy indifference to formulas and categories. This very elusiveness is not only a very great charm, but furnishes evidence of the important part which wit and humour play in human affairs. They are omnipresent : they register the overflow of the soul in art, religion, and history ; merriment and sorrow, friendship and animosity, purity and evil, have found common use in them. No qualities are better known, or more readily recognizable ; but they are still at large. They will never be caught in any snare of definition, however skilfully set. We shall delight in their manifestations, use them as part of our common speech, value them among the greater resources of life ; but we shall never define them as we define a thing fixed and stationary, or a relation the contacts of which are seen on all sides. Wit is too

Protean, humour too elemental, for complete definition. This is not saying that deep glimpses into the
nature of these qualities are lacking, or that acute and
luminous comments on the differences between them
have not been made. English literature, which is nota-
bly rich in both wit and humour, is also rich in illustration and characterization of these qualities. Hazlitt,
Leigh Hunt, and Thackeray have approved themselves
as commentators whose joy was in the text rather than
in the comment; while of the large company of English and American essayists and critics there are few
who have not made some contribution to a clearer
understanding of these fugitive things.

Exact definition is not, however, the prerequisite of
deep thinking, or of a really profound comprehension
either of the things of the spirit or of the mind; if it
were, we should be cut off from dealing intelligently
with the things which are nearest and most essential
to us. The deepest things in our lives are best known
and least definable. As soon as we touch them, we
slip out of logic into poetry.

Wit, being distinctively an intellectual quality, presents sharper outlines than humour; but the two qualities so often appear together that, at the first glance,
they seem to be interchangeable. They have, indeed,
this characteristic in common : they arise out of the
perception of some kind of incongruity, some form
of contrast. Wit is lighter, drier, more distinctly
localized, more purely intellectual, than humour; and
humour is more elemental, more pervasive, more a

matter of character and temperament. Wit is allied to talent in its cleverness, dexterity, and a certain hard and brilliant quality of skill; while humour partakes of the wider reach, the ampler flow, the deep unconsciousness of genius. Wit is the swift play, the flashing thrust and parry, of the mind. Humour flows from character; its springs are in a man's nature; it is the expression, not of that which is rapid, dexterous, and self-conscious, but of that which is fundamental and unconscious in him. Wit is a thing apart from character; humour is the most unforced expression of character. The old physicians were not far wrong in making humour one of the four elements out of which the physical body is compounded, and therefore part of the very substance of a man. This original use of the word is the most suggestive comment on its meaning; we shall not go astray if we follow its lead. It was one of those instinctive guesses which fuller knowledge has verified in quite unexpected fashion. Wit plays on the surface of things; humour streams down into the heart of them, irradiates them, and, without intention, gets at their secret. Wit is colourless, emotionless; it is as dry, as detached from the things it touches, as an abstract quality. Humour, being the expression of the whole nature, is full of heart; it has tenderness, sympathy, piety, sadness; the laughter which it evokes is without malice or bitterness; it is often so near to tears that the two blend as naturally as the moods of an April sky.

The deepest humour is never cynical or destructive;

it never wounds. The wit of Voltaire is often but the
mask of a sneer, and the wit of Heine cuts like the
surgeon's blade ; but the humour of Cervantes is full
of reverence and courtesy, and the humour of Shakespeare of human tenderness and sadness.

Dr. Bushnell brings out the fundamental quality
of each when he says : " One is the dry labour of
intention or design, ambition eager to provoke applause, malignity biting at an adversary, envy letting
down the good or the exalted. The other, humour,
is the soul reeking with its own moisture, laughing because it is full of laughter, — as ready to weep as to
laugh ; for the copious shower it holds is good for
either. And then, when it has set the tree a-dripping,

> ' And hung a pearl in every cowslip's ear,'

the pure sun shining after will reveal no colour of
intention in the sparkling drop, but will leave you
doubting still whether it be a drop let fall by laughter
or a tear." Spontaneity and health of soul are the
characteristics of humour. Wit may be spontaneous ;
humour must be. Wit may be sound and sweet ;
humour must be. Wit may let us into the secret of
character ; humour must reveal it.

The great wits form a sharply-defined group of ver-
satile and gifted persons, not so often read as quoted ;
for by its very nature wit is a portable rather than a
diffusive quality. It reveals itself in sudden flashes,
not in a continuous glow and illumination. It is distilled in sentences ; it is preserved in figures, illustra-

tions, epigrams, epithets, phrases. In these days one reads Voltaire and Sydney Smith for " points," not for broad completeness or for large and luminous disclosure of the nature of the themes with which they deal. The elder Dumas has stamped his superscription on a few pieces of the pure gold of wit, which furnish a standard coinage among the most critical and fastidious. Heine's rare poetic insight and unique quality are too often undervalued in comparison with that arrowy wit,—never barbed with bitterness, and yet always left stinging in the victim as if dipped in the very essence of malice. Wit seems, upon analysis, a conversational quality, called out by social relations and influences, and expressed briefly and compactly, with the incisiveness of epigram and repartee. It is the sharpest of comments ; it often brings a ray of most intense light to bear on a defect, an exaggeration, a falsehood : but it does not deal with subjects broadly and comprehensively ; it does not illuminate wide fields of thought and life ; it has no creative quality ; there is nothing elemental in it. It is like the flash of lightning during the brief duration of which a bit of landscape stands out in startling distinctness ; it has none of the wide, fruitful, revealing quality of the sunlight.

The great humorists present a significant contrast to the great wits ; for while the wits entertain and dazzle us, the humorists reveal life to us. Aristophanes, Cervantes, Molière, and Shakespeare, the typical humorists, are among the greatest contributors to the capital of human achievement. They give us, not glimpses, but views of life, — not detached comments, but comprehensive interpretations. They are pre-eminently creative ; and the ease and breadth of their work hint at the elemental quality of humour. A humorist of the first order has always great range, and moves freely through an almost limitless world of thought and fancy. In his most destructive moods, Aristophanes gives forth such an impression of force and compass that in the very process of decomposing one world, he seems to be constructing another. Lucian has far less fertility and resource of imagination, less buoyancy and splendour of poetic fancy ; but he also moves at ease in a world ampler than that of his contemporaries, — a world which his humour, even when destructive of the old faith, broadens rather than destroys. Rabelais, in the broadest spirit of license, makes an honest fight for more reality and less sham, — for a wider and freer world. Cervantes, Molière, and Heine, with very different gifts, and from very different points of view, share this quality of overflowing abundance and vitality. There is no consciousness of strain in them, — no evident effort to conform to certain standards and to meet certain tests. On the contrary, they move in an atmosphere of free and independent expression ; they are continually breaking through the imaginary conventional limits of their time, and breaking into a larger world. The arid and ludicrous formalism of the chivalric habit after the spirit of chivalry has fled ; typical hypocrisies and specious self-deceit; the stupidity and dense self-satisfaction of Philistinism, — all these various forms of narrowness and falsehood are limitations of human growth and free activity; and against these limitations the humorists break their lances. Heine justly claimed for himself the position of a liberator of humanity; for all the great humorists are liberators.

It is true that Aristophanes, Lucian, and Heine are often distinctly destructive in mood, and seem to have no other purpose but to make current beliefs incredible. Heine, the most volatile and tricksy spirit in literature, slips into blasphemy with magical ease, and is never so far from seriousness of spirit as when he puts himself most completely under the spell of sentiment. "Other bards," says a writer in a recent issue of the "Atheneum," "have passed from grave to gay within the compass of one work; but the art of constantly showing two natures within the small limit of perhaps three ballad verses was reserved for Heine. No one like him understands how to build up a little edifice of the tenderest and most refined sentiment for the mere pleasure of knocking it down with a last line. No one like him approaches his reader with doleful countenance, pours into the ear a tale of secret sorrow, and when the sympathies are enlisted surprises his confidant with a horse-laugh. It seems as though Nature had endowed him with a most delicate sensibility and a keen perception of the ridiculous, that his own feelings may afford him a perpetual subject for banter." This incessant intermingling of the most delicate feeling with the broadest or keenest satire was, of course, temperamental; no one has ever passed from one mood to the other so swiftly as Heine. But the transition is characteristic of all the great humorists. One does not need to read Heine very thoroughly to discover that there is a constant struggle in his soul, — a struggle to break with Hebraism, and reconcile himself with Hellenism. He revolts against the Hebrew spirit, because it seems to rob him of a goodly portion of life; to recover the beauty and harmony which seem to have perished with the Greeks is at once the endeavour and the pang of his life. It is this consciousness of dissonance which inspires the spirit of mockery in him. He cannot feel at home in his own time; it limits him, hinders him, binds him; it is, in his feeling at least, too small for him. Consciously or unconsciously, he is always fighting against limitations and striving after a broader life. This is the deeper significance of his work, as it is the deepest significance of humour.

For that which was true of Heine was still more true of Aristophanes, — the most audacious of all the humorists. It was Heine himself who said : " A deep idea of world-destruction lies at the root of every Aristophanic comedy, and, like a fantastically ironical magic-tree, springs up in it with blooming ornaments of thought, with singing nightingales, and climbing, chattering apes ; " and he speaks elsewhere of the Aristophanic "jubilee of death and fire-works of annihilation." The sweep of Aristophanes's imagination, the license of his fancy, the depth and beauty of his thought, the lawless audacity of his satire, give an impression of fathomless scepticism, — the searching irony of a god looking on human life from the standpoint of cynical indifference. He handles his materials with a kind of Olympian breadth and ease, — more like a god creating worlds out of his own surplusage of vitality than like a satirist. It is highly improbable that he was the deliberate and conscious moralist which some of his German students and critics have held him to be ; but the vein of seriousness in his work is quite as evident as the vein of poetry ; and in a certain swift and splendid effectiveness, no poet has ever surpassed him. To his most careless reader he conveys a sense of freedom, an idea of breadth and vastness, which are at times almost overwhelming. He moves in the creative element ; his influence plays like fire upon the habits, beliefs, and vices which seemed to him corrupt, false, or ridiculous. His work was, in its ultimate effect, the work of a liberator.

If this expansive quality of humour, this liberating force, is characteristic of the destructive humorists, it is still more notable and significant in the constructive humorists, — those who, like Shakespeare, Molière, Cervantes, Richter, and Carlyle, have dealt with life with broad or genial earnestness and sincerity. The study of both schools of humour brings out clearly the very significant fact that humour in-

volves the background of a greater world than that
in which the humorists sport. Carlyle says of Socrates
that he was " terribly at ease in Zion ; " he handled
life and its deepest concerns with an ease and freedom which betray a consciousness of being at home
amid the mysteries of existence and, in a way, superior to them. That is the attitude of the great
humorist : he plays with life in the sense in which
play implies greater range and freedom than work.
For while work involves a certain subjection of the
man to his toil, a certain submission of the artisan to
the task, play implies ease, freedom, and fulness.
Play is the spontaneous overflow of a great force, the
natural and painless putting forth of strength, the
delight and fertility of the artist handling his material as the plastic medium of his thought.

The rigid logician, refusing the aid of insight and
rejecting the imagination as untrustworthy, stands
under the shadow of the globe, and bends, like an
over-laden Atlas, under the appalling weight of the
burden. He moves within fixed limits, along prescribed paths, — often with passionate eagerness and
intensity of spirit, but oblivious of all sides of life
save the one upon which the thought is fixed, and with
the air of one passing over dangerous territory and
dreading solicitation or attack. The humorist, on
the other hand, stands aside from the world, and
watches its movement as part of a greater order ;
studies it with an audacious ease and equipoise ;
judges it with the assurance of one whose vision in-

cludes the whole of which it is part. He feels its suffering and recognizes its tragic elements; but in his broad conception the shadows are relieved by the lights, and the gloom of the parts is swallowed up in the brightness of the whole. For while the humorist is often a pessimist so far as immediate conditions are concerned, he is an optimist in his faith in the reality of the universe and the dignity and worth of life in its completeness.

Socrates was at ease and could play at times ironically with matters of apparently deepest moment, because, beyond all local and racial beliefs, he had the resource of a fundamental faith. Carlyle, whose humour and imagination so constantly acted and reacted upon each other, made traditions and conventions pitiful or absurd, by evoking that background of infinity and eternity against which all human life is set. Shakespeare's tragic power is found, in the last analysis, to be one with his comic power; both flow from his nature and his view of life. He deals with the tragic forces as one who is superior to them; for they are, in fact, inimical only to those who offend against the laws whose servants they are. He describes their operation, and records their appalling results with no lack of that fundamental seriousness which is the mood of every profound nature, but with the calmness and quietude of soul that come from the ability to look beyond the passing blackness and fury of the storm into the heavens which they obscure for the moment, only to make their serenity and purity the more apparent. Speaking reverently, there is something of the divine repose in the greatest humour, — the repose which comes from a vision of the totality of things.

Humour in this elemental sense is the perception of those contrasts and incongruities which are a part of the very texture of human life. From the standpoint of a formally logical view of life this contrast is pathetic and even tragic ; from the standpoint of the large, free interpretation of faith, through the imagination, this contrast is full of humour. From the divine point of view, there is the same element of humour in human life which the mature mind finds in those experiences of childhood which are painful, because they arise from ignorance of the relative duration and importance of things. There is, as an acute thinker has pointed out, something fundamentally humorous in the very conditions of human life ; in the spectacle of immortal souls becoming merchants and trafficking in all manner of perishable wares, and of these same imperishable souls spending energy and heart in a struggle to feed and clothe a body which is but the shell of the spirit. Humour has its source in this fundamental contrast between the human soul, with its far-reaching relations and its immortality, and the conditions of its mortal life. This elemental humour has had no more striking expression of late years than in "Sartor Resartus," — a work of genius conceived in the deepest spirit of humour, and finding its theme in the contrast between a spirit and the clothes which it wears. "To the eye of vulgar Logic," says Teufelsdröckh, "what is man? An omnivorous Biped that wears Breeches. To the eye of Pure Reason what is he? A Soul, a Spirit, and divine Apparition. Round his mysterious ME, there lies, under all those wool-rags, a Garment of Flesh (or of Senses) contextured in the Loom of Heaven; whereby he is revealed to his like, and dwells with them in Union and Division; and sees and fashions for himself a Universe, with azure Starry Spaces, and long Thousands of Years. Deep-hidden is he under that strange Garment; amid Sounds and Colours and Forms, as it were, swathed-in and inextricably over-shrouded: yet it is sky-woven, and worthy of a God. Stands he not thereby in the centre of Immensities, in the conflux of Eternities?"

This contrast between the Finite and the Infinite is the source of the deep and sane humour which is shared by all the creative minds. For it is significant that, with the possible exception of Dante, all the greatest men have been richly endowed with this quality, and the Italians claim it for Dante. If life is long enough and comprehensive enough to provide for the final reconcilement of apparent contradictions, and the final adjustment of all just claims for opportunity and happiness, then humour becomes a prophecy of the joyful outcome of all struggles and incongruities, and of the final resolution of all discords into harmony. In natures of the widest range, this fundamental faith seems to be implicit in the consciousness; it lies below all thinking, and

gives it ease, freedom, and the sportiveness of childhood, which plays serenely in the presence of the
sublimest forces, not through insensibility, but through
confidence in the benignity of the universal order.
The narrower, severer minds, like Calvin, — following
rigidly logical processes, and shutting a large part
of life out of the field of vision, — are not only
partial and inadequate interpreters of life, but seem
to be always desperately contending against atheism;
the large, sunny, poetic natures, on the other hand,
have such rootage in essential faith that, without loss
of moral earnestness, they can deal with the contrasts
of human history in the free, confident spirit of
humour. If the mistake which the boy makes in his
Latin grammar involves permanent ignorance, there
is an element of sadness in it; but if it is to be succeeded ultimately by mastery of the subject, it is
humorous, and we smile at it. If the grief at some
small loss is as final and lasting as it appears to a
child, it is sad enough; but if it is soon to be forgotten, if, later, a fuller knowledge is to reveal an
exaggeration of emotion, then the exaggeration becomes humorous, and we smile at the recollection.
If life be as great as our highest hopes, many
of our present sorrows must have this ignorance
of relative importance in them; however real and
painful they are, they must present to an intelligence
higher than ours an element of exaggeration. If the
contrast between Finite and the Infinite, between
Real and the Ideal, is permanent, then the life of men

is the saddest, hardest, and most bitter existence imaginable. If, on the other hand, these contrasts are the contrasts between different stages of a successful development ; if contradiction, incongruity, and imperfection are passing phases in a progression toward final harmony, — then the life of man permits of the freedom, the delight, the confidence, of secure and happy childhood. The sanest souls instinctively believe their noblest conception of the range and significance of life ; and because they believe, humour springs up like a fountain of joy in them. And so humour of the highest kind becomes the truest evidence of that fundamental faith which lays its foundations deeper than all systems of dogma. The humorists are always struggling for a broader world, because they believe that such a world exists.

The part which humour plays as a refuge from crushing care and calamity, a resource under the pressure of responsibilities too heavy to be borne, is not clearly recognized save by the few who have given thought to the subject. There is a general impression that humour involves levity, and that the man who permits it to play for a moment in the clouds which overshadow him is lacking in seriousness of nature, or is oblivious of the deeper aspects of his surroundings. This impression is the very reverse of the truth ; for humour of the highest quality is never far from sadness, and is always allied with fundamental gravity of character. Humour is not the resource of men of levity and superficial views of life ; it is the resource of men in whose temperaments the tragical note is dominant, and who feel too keenly the pressure of the tragic element. Edwin Booth writes of his father : " For a like reason would my father open, so to speak, the safety-valve of levity in some of his most impassioned moments. At the instant of intense emotion, when the spectators were enthralled by his magnetic influence, the tragedian's overwrought brain would take refuge from its own threatening storm beneath the jester's hood, and, while turned from the audience, he would whisper some silliness, or ' make a face.' When he left the stage, however, no allusion to such seeming frivolity was permitted. His fellow-actors who perceived these trivialities ignorantly attributed his conduct at such times to lack of feeling ; whereas it was extreme excess of feeling which thus forced his brain back from the very verge of madness."

The name of Booth suggests another name which has become synonymous with both tragedy and humour. There were many to whom Mr. Lincoln's humour, in those terrible years of strain and struggle, seemed not only a violation of good taste, but a kind of irreverence. They did not recognize the pathos of that lonely and over-burdened life, the sadness of that great and solitary nature. Humour was something more than a resource to Mr. Lincoln ; it was the safeguard of sanity. It was the relaxation of the tension of mind which made the preservation of the mental equilibrium pos-

sible ; it was the momentary play of the heart breaking
away from the appalling problems with which the intellect was constantly dealing, and from which, for
long intervals of time, there seemed no escape. It
was the sudden reassurance of the spirit almost over-
borne by the responsibilities which rested upon it ;
the swift flight of the soul out of the storm into the
serenity beyond the circle of its ravages. There was
fundamental faith in it.

THE END.